ACKNOWLEDGEMENTS

The research consultant would like to thank the local researchers who undertook interviews with offenders and agencies and who extracted data from court records: Jean Craig (Highland), Ahmed Andrews (Tayside) and Brent Hodgson (Ayr). We are also grateful to the SAO staff who provided data from their records for research purposes and the court staff who accessed the necessary court records, especially as each of these staff were very busy with their own duties. Finally, the researcher would like to thank those who gave up their time to provide their views on the scheme: the sentencers, clerks of court, SAO staff and managers, agencies providing activities and the SAO offenders.

CONTENTS

Page

1. INTRODUCTION

    A. Background   1
    B. Aims and Objectives of the Supervised Attendance Order   1
    C. Description of the Schemes   3
    D. Research Objectives & Methodology   8
    E. Social Work Department Liaison with Courts (pre-pilot)   10
    Conclusion   11

2. THE IMPACT OF THE SAO ON SENTENCING PRACTICES

    A. Background   13
    B. Fines and Default   13
    C. Rate of Attendance at FECs   15
    D. Court Disposals   16
    E. District Courts   18
    Conclusion   19

3. MONITORING OF THE PILOT SCHEMES

    A. Number of Hours and Tariff   21
    B. Characteristics of Defaulters   22
    C. Court Procedures and Practices   25
    D. SAO Procedures and Practices   30
    Conclusion   32

4. EVALUATION OF THE PILOT SCHEMES

    A. Objectives of the SAO   34
    B. Operational Objectives   40
    Conclusion   42

5. EVALUATION OF THE GUIDELINES

    Legislation and Method of Introduction   44
    The National Guidelines   45
    Activities for Offenders   47
    Working Arrangements   47
    Requirements of the Order and Compliance   48
    Monitoring and Evaluation   48

6. CONCLUSION   49

LIST OF TABLES AND DIAGRAMS

		Page
Table I.	Those Fined as a Proportion of Those with Charge Proved	13
Table II.	Rate of Default	14
Table III.	Age of Defaulters and All Those Fined (Dundee Sheriff Court)	14
Table IV.	Amount of Fine Outstanding	15
Table V.	Warrants for Non-Attendance	15
Table VI.	Disposals of Fine Defaulters by Court and Year	16
Table VII.	Number of SAO Hours by Court	21
Table VIII.	Balance of Fine by SAO Hours	22
Table IX.	Completion of SA Hours and SA Orders	22
Table X.	Age of Those Given SAO and Custody and All Attenders	23
Table XI.	Previous Sentences of SAO Offenders	24
Table XII.	Number of SAOs as a Rate Per 100 Attenders	25
Table XIII.	Number of Orders Since Start of Each Scheme	26
Table XIV.	Number of SAOs in the First Year	27
Table XV.	Unacceptable Absences	31
Table XVI.	Fine Defaulters: Receptions into Custody and Custodial Sentences and Alternatives by Year and Court.	35
Diagram I.	Previous Sentences of SAO and Custody Offenders, Ayr	24

SUMMARY OF RESEARCH FINDINGS

Chapter 1 describes the background to the Supervised Attendance Order, the research aims and methods and the establishment and characteristics of the pilot schemes. The Supervised Attendance order (SAO) was introduced in Scotland under Section 62 of the Law Reform (Miscellaneous Provisions) (Scotland) Act 1990. The aim of the Supervised Attendance Order is to reduce the number and proportion of offenders sent to prison or detention as a result of their being in default of a fine. Supervised Attendance is an order of a Scottish criminal court whereby a fine defaulter is required to attend such places and undertake such activities as instructed by the supervising social work officer for a specified time of between 10 and 60 hours. A court can make a SAO only after it has decided at that time not to remit the fine, allow further time to pay, reduce the level of instalments or change the length of the intervals between instalment payments. The court must consider the SAO more appropriate than the imposition of a period of imprisonment.

The Scottish Office decided that a few pilot schemes should be monitored and evaluated prior to decisions about whether the SAO should be extended into other areas. The three schemes selected for the pilot were South Ayrshire (Ayr Sheriff Court), Tayside (Dundee and Perth Sheriff and District Courts) and Highland (Inverness, Tain and Dingwall Sheriff Courts). Each scheme has developed a different model in relation to the type of activities offered and the management of the scheme.

During the period of research fieldwork (June 1992 to January 1993), the Supervised Attendance activities in Ayr were either educational or 'constructive use of time' (such as leisure and recreation). The local community (via local organisations) is actively involved in the provision and presentation of activities, some of which are presented and supervised by SAO staff.

The Tayside scheme's activities were mainly educational and 'constructive use of time', with some offenders undertaking unpaid work in the community. The SAO staff of the social work department undertake the statutory duties in relation to supervision of the Order and APEX (Scotland), a voluntary organisation concerned with retraining or assisting offenders to obtain employment, is responsible for the organisational and delivery aspects of the Order. During the research period local organisations and businesses provided some opportunities for unpaid work.

The Highland scheme can perhaps be viewed as a mini community service scheme which offers only unpaid work (often identical to that undertaken by offenders on a Community Service Order) which is supervised by community service supervisors. The scheme is managed by social work staff who are also responsible for the administration of Community Service Orders.

The aims of the research are to monitor and evaluate the establishment and operation of the pilot schemes and the national guidelines, to assist revision of the guidelines into National Standards and to inform the design of further schemes. The research objectives are:

- To monitor the establishment of the schemes

- To describe the use currently being made by courts in the pilot schemes of imprisonment and of alternatives to imprisonment for fine default.

- To monitor the pilot schemes and evaluate the operational effectiveness and value of the national guidelines.

- To evaluate the efficiency and effectiveness of the pilot schemes in terms of the objectives set out by the national guidelines.

The research methodology included:

- Interviews with sentencers, clerks to the courts and social work department officers prior to the commencement of schemes (which, for most schemes, was August or September 1992).

- Extraction of data from Fines Enquiry Court[1] lists between 1989 and 1991 and from lists of courts sitting from the start of each scheme until the end of January 1993.

- Extraction of data within and attached to the complaint.

- Extraction of data from social work and SAO records relating to the activities undertaken, attendance and behaviour.

- Interviews with sentencers, clerks to the courts, SAO staff and agencies providing activities, at the end of the period of fieldwork.

- Interviews with offenders on completion of their Order and, during February 1993, interviews with offenders who had completed at least 10 hours.

- A self-completion questionnaire for those sentencers, clerks and offenders who were unable or unwilling to be interviewed.

Chapter 2 examines the impact of the SAO on sentencing practices. As this research was conducted during the initial stages of the new court disposal and covered only a few months of operation (between four and seven months) when numbers of Orders imposed were relatively low, the results can only provide an indication of how SAOs might influence sentencing practice in the future once a greater number of Orders will have been imposed. Dundee District Court was found to differ from the sheriff courts in many aspects, such as having the highest proportion of female defaulters, the highest use of the fine and the least frequent use of the custodial sentence for default. There was some evidence that the introduction of the SAO may have reduced the proportion receiving a custodial sentence at Ayr Sheriff Court. Further research is required to assess whether this effect will be sustained in Ayr and whether it will become evident in other schemes after the initial stages of operation.

---

[1]Although the terminology 'Means Enquiry Court' (MEC) is more common, the Criminal Justice (Scotland) Act 1980 changed this to 'Fines Enquiry Court' (FEC).

The monitoring of the scheme is covered in **Chapter 3** and the main findings include:

- In all courts, those aged under 21 were over-represented amongst offenders on a SAO compared to all defaulters attending courts and those receiving a custodial sentence for default.

- Over two-thirds of all offenders on a SAO had been fined before and over one quarter had previous experience of custody.

- Numbers of SAOs imposed were lower than expected in each scheme and there appeared to be a need to remind sentencers about SAOs and inform all visiting sentencers of the existence of this new court disposal.

- Sentencers' estimates of the proportion of offenders on a SAO who might previously have received a custodial sentence ranged from none to 100%.

- By the end of January 1993 only one case had been breached and a further five applications for breach had been made but had not yet been heard in court.

Chapter 4 presents an evaluation of the pilot schemes within the constraints of low numbers of SAOs and the brief period covered by the research. Despite these problems, several measures of success can be identified:

- Orders are being made and successfully completed.

- An analysis of court records showed that the SAO seems to be used as an alternative to custody in Ayr.

- The views of the SAO staff suggest that SAOs are being used as an alternative to custody in over three-quarters of all cases.

- The majority of receptions to custody for fine default are as a result of the imposition of the alternative on subsequent default after more time to pay.

- The number of unacceptable absences as a rate per 100 completed hours is very low (between 3 and 8) in all courts, except for the Perth courts (27).

- Discipline is being imposed on offenders - unacceptable absences and behaviour are resulting in formal warnings and breach is being invoked.

- Sentencers, overall, consider the activities to be constructive and the Order to be credible.

- The majority of offenders considered that they would rather have a SAO than a custodial sentence or more time to pay, would agree to undertake a SAO in the future and felt that they had learnt something.

Chapter 5 deals with the evaluation of the effectiveness of the guidelines and comments on the legislation. SAO staff and sentencers made a few suggestions for change in the guidelines such as: the inclusion of a tariff scale; an acknowledgement of the expectation of a slow start-up; the importance of reminding sentencers and solicitors of the availability of the SAO; and a reduction in the interval between an absence and its follow-up. Some important issues were raised and remain to be resolved:

- There was some support amongst sentencers, SAO staff and offenders for the introduction of the SAO as a primary disposal.

- It was suggested that the 10-hour core module could perhaps be dispersed throughout the order to ease the problem of the irregular flow of orders and to vary the type of activities experienced by the offenders in a short period.

- Policy makers should consider whether the three different models (which were claimed by the social work departments to reflect the geographical characteristics of each area) should continue or whether these differences might undermine the identity of the SAO and that a more limited range of models should operate in the future.

Although it is recognised that the number of Orders imposed by the end of the research period was rather low and did not allow for a rigorous evaluation (which would be more appropriate at a later stage once numbers have increased and more experience gained), overall, the monitoring and evaluation of the pilot schemes concluded that this is a viable community-based disposal.

1. INTRODUCTION

A. Background

1.1   The Supervised Attendance Order (SAO) was introduced as an alternative to custody for fine defaulters under Section 62 of the Law Reform (Miscellaneous Provisions) (Scotland) Act 1990. The Act enables a court to make a SAO only after it has decided at that time not to remit the fine, allow further time for payment, reduce the level of instalments or lengthen the intervals between instalment payments and the court must consider the SAO more appropriate than the imposition of a period of imprisonment. Supervised Attendance is an order of a Scottish criminal court whereby a fine defaulter is required to attend such places and undertake and participate in such activities as instructed by the supervising social work officer for a specified time of 10, 20, 30, 40, 50 or 60 hours.

1.2   The origins of the SAO were rooted in the general concern about the high proportion of the prison population who were fine defaulters,[1] particularly those whose offences tended to be less serious than those receiving a custodial sentence in the first instance[2].

1.3   Fines have continued to be by far the most common court disposal and have consistently remained at 75 to 79 per cent of all disposals of persons with charge proved between 1985 and 1992. The reception of fine defaulters as a rate per 1000 persons fined fluctuated between 74 and 79 until 1987 then decreased to 71 and 70 in 1988 and 1989 but decreased dramatically to 52 in 1990, increasing again to 61 in 1991 and 63 in 1992.

1.4   The high rate of receptions to custody on default of all those fined (although the rate in recent years has been less than the 1980's), has prompted the demand for an alternative to custody for this large group of offenders. The Scottish Office consulted regional and district councils, courts, legal establishments and other interested parties about the most appropriate alternative to custody for fine defaulters, resulting in the Supervised Attendance Order (Section 62 of the Law Reform (Miscellaneous Provisions) (Scotland) Act 1990).

B.   Aims and Objectives of the Supervised Attendance Order

1.5   The aim of the SAO is to reduce the number and proportion of offenders sent to prison or detention as a result of their being in default of a fine. The objectives of the SAO are:

- To provide Scottish criminal courts with a credible community based penalty which may be used as an alternative to prison or detention for offenders who default in the payment of a fine.

- To provide offenders in default of payment of a fine an opportunity to receive a community based penalty instead of serving a period of imprisonment or detention.

---

[1] Between 1985 and 1989, 45 per cent to 49 per cent of receptions to penal establishments were for fine default but this proportion dropped to 40 per cent in 1990, 43 per cent in 1991 and 42 per cent in 1992 (Source: The Scottish Office "Prison Statistics Scotland" Bulletins).

[2] Between 42 and 49 per cent of fine defaulter receptions to penal establishments in 1985-1992 related to fines for crimes as opposed to offences, which is much less than the rate for direct receptions of whom 73 to 76 per cent were fined for crimes as opposed to offences. (Source: The Scottish Office "Prison Statistics Scotland" Bulletins).

- To ensure SAOs are characterised by the imposition of discipline, firm and reliable supervision and that activities are constructive.

1.6   Supervised Attendance is intended to be a low cost order entailing minimum assessment and with participation in group activity.   No pre-sentence suitability assessment or report is required, although the offender's consent is required before an order can be made. The intention is to provide a time penalty in substitution for a fine but to use the time constructively.   It is in effect, a fine on the offender's time.

1.7   Offenders are liable to disciplinary procedures when they fail to comply with requirements relating to the following without reasonable cause:

- Failure to attend for activity as instructed.

- Lack of punctuality.

- Failure to report as required to the supervising social work officer.

- Failure to notify a change of address without delay.

- Failure to notify a change in employment circumstances without delay.

- Failure to perform the activity satisfactorily (regarding drugs, alcohol, smoking and health and safety and satisfactory behaviour).

1.8   Absences must be followed up within four working days of notification and the offender should, wherever possible, be interviewed for this purpose.   The supervising officer has discretion about when to invoke formal disciplinary procedures when other requirements are not met. When the supervising officer decides that an explanation offered by the offender for failure to attend is unacceptable or that formal disciplinary action should be taken for other reasons, a formal warning is given to the offender either orally or in writing on the first occasion, a final warning is issued on the second occasion and on the third occasion, breach proceedings are instituted.

1.9   The Social Work Services Group of the Home and Health Department developed the 'National Guidelines for the Operation of Supervised Attendance Orders in Scotland' as a guide for regions about to establish a SAO in their area.   Regional Council Social Work Departments were invited to submit proposals for establishing a Supervised Attendance Order scheme and three were selected as pilot schemes (Tayside, Highland and South Ayrshire). It was decided that these pilot schemes should be monitored and evaluated prior to decisions about whether the SAO should be extended to other areas, how Supervised Attendance should be developed and to assist in the revision of the Guidelines into National Standards.

1.10   It was originally intended that all schemes should commence on 1st March 1992 but delays resulted in Supervised Attendance Orders being introduced on different dates in the three pilot areas.   (Since January 1993, SAOs have been extended to other courts within each area). The courts included in the research study commenced on the following dates:

Tain Sheriff	(Highland scheme)	22 June 1992
Dingwall Sheriff	(Highland scheme)	22 June 1992
Dundee Sheriff	(Tayside scheme)	14 July 1992
Dundee District	(Tayside scheme)	14 July 1992
Inverness Sheriff	(Highland scheme)	3 August 1992
Ayr Sheriff	(Ayrshire scheme)	22September1992
Perth Sheriff	(Tayside scheme)	2 November 1992
Perth District	(Tayside scheme)	2 November 1992

C.   Description of the Schemes

1.11   This section provides a summary description of each scheme.   More details are contained in Chapter 3 'Monitoring of The Pilot Schemes'.   The three pilot schemes have each adopted a different model of operation of the SAO which, to a certain extent, relate to the demographic features of each area.   Demographic characteristics have been obtained to assess whether and in what way these have had any influence on the operation and ultimate 'success' of SAO schemes and whether they should be taken into consideration when establishing and developing schemes. For example, one might expect that schemes in rural areas where a few offenders on a SAO are scattered throughout a wide geographic area, would require to be organised in a different way from an urban scheme which might have a more regular flow and greater number of offenders at any one time.

1.12   The population served by the sheriff courts in the study varies considerably.   Dundee Sheriff Court serves 165,873, Ayr Sheriff Court 155,252 and Highland 111,383[1] (as the number of SAOs in the three sheriff courts in Highland are so low, it was decided to analyse figures from these courts together).   Both the Ayr and Highland schemes include urban areas but they also cover a wide rural area resulting in problems of frequency and cost of public transport, travel time and setting up groups in different centres.

The South Ayrshire Scheme

(i)   Staffing and Accommodation

1.13   The South Ayrshire scheme is run by one full-time Supervised Attendance Organiser (senior social worker level) and one full-time Supervised Attendance Assistant (social work

---

[1]1991 Census

assistant grade), both of whom report to the District Co-ordinator (Offenders) who reports to the District Officer. Area teams are not involved in the management of SAOs. The Supervised Attendance Organiser and Assistant receive support from a full-time clerical assistant. The responsibilities of the Supervised Attendance Organiser and Assistant include the post-sentence interview with the offender which takes place on the same day as the Supervised Attendance Order is imposed and lasts about one hour which was initially credited to the SAO hours but is no longer credited. This interview covers an explanation of Supervised Attendance and assessment of the offender's needs, such as childminding, health, addictions etc and family and employment commitments. SAO staff are also responsible for presentation of some of the educational activities, liaison with the agencies providing supervision of the other activities and responsibility for following up instances of non-compliance and applications to court for breach.

1.14   Activities are provided at two main centres, one in Ayr and one in Cumnock (16 miles west of Ayr). From January 1993, some activities were also provided at Girvan (22 miles south of Ayr) to avoid offenders having to travel an hour each way to reach Ayr. The accommodation in New Road, Ayr provides two offices for the SAO staff and shared access with other social work department sections to two large rooms for activities. Two rooms are rented within Barrhill Community Centre, Cumnock for Supervised Attendance activities for people from that area. As there is generally a poor bus service early in the morning and in an attempt to avoid high non-attendance rates (Community Service in Ayr has the second highest breach rate in Scotland and it was suggested that this was partly due to offenders being picked up at 7.45 am at the weekend resulting in many missing the bus), most sessions are arranged for the afternoon. Evening sessions finish before 9.30pm to let offenders catch the last buses or trains.

(ii)   Types of Offender and Activities (Ayrshire)

1.15   The scheme aims to be flexible to accommodate the needs of employed offenders (providing evening and weekend activities), single parents (assisting in paying for a childminder if necessary - providing a creche was considered to be too expensive) and those with other special needs. The accommodation for group activities are all on the ground floor and would be accessible to those with a physical disability. Supervisors would be informed of those with literacy problems and activity programmes would take these into account.

1.16   The District Co-ordinator (Offenders) asked area teams for a list of organisations in their area who might have something to offer the SAO programme and these organisations were invited to put forward their own ideas. In addition to ongoing liaison with each organisation, all organisations were invited to attend a meeting to discuss their plans in detail. There was no difficulty in finding a wide range of appropriate agencies who were prepared to offer relevant sessions for the offenders on a SAO. During the four months up to the end of January 1993, 11 voluntary organisations, local authority or health agencies had provided activities for offenders on a SAO. Negotiations with a further nine agencies were continuing or had been completed by the end of the research period.

4

1.17 The model adopted by the South Ayrshire scheme, which follows the Social Work Services Group guidelines closely, provides a 10-hour core module of educational activities (covering health; education and leisure; education and employment; and money advice and debt) presented by the SAO staff and those offenders with more than a 10-hour Order can choose further more in-depth sessions from these four areas which will be presented by local agencies. SAO staff carry out initial assessments during the core module and if necessary, would direct offenders in their choice of activity by suggesting areas in which they needed more in-depth advice or help. The final decision is negotiated between the SAO staff and the offender. Unpaid work is not a feature of this model. The specific topics covered by SAO staff and the agencies include:

- debt and money advice
- attitudes and offending behaviour
- risk and decision-making
- employment and training
- victim support
- safety
- alcohol, drugs and AIDS education
- welfare rights
- stress, health
- consumer rights
- assertiveness training
- community involvement
- constructive use of leisure time
- computing
- a first aid course

1.18 In practice, the lower than expected number of SAOs imposed, the varying flow of orders per month and the distribution of offenders between three centres (which meant that few offenders from the one locality were at the same stage in their order), resulted in the temporary suspension of the policy that all offenders must undertake the 10-hour core module before undertaking other modules. It was hoped that the original policy could be reintroduced once numbers increased (although all offenders undertake most of the core module activities at some point during their order).

(iii)   Supervision, Discipline and Breach (Ayrshire)

1.19 The policy is that offenders will be supervised by the two SAO staff at core modules and by one SAO staff and one agency representative at the advanced modules. Absences will result in a home visit by one SAO staff within 48 hours if possible. Absences will be considered acceptable if the offender has gained previous permission, has a medical certificate or proves a genuine emergency. All other absences will be classified as unacceptable.

1.20 The proposed procedures for discipline and breach follow the Social Work Services Group guidelines. For example, one unacceptable absence or instance of unacceptable behaviour will result in a formal warning letter. Unacceptable behaviour includes smoking outwith designated times and areas, swearing, poor punctuality and general poor behaviour. On the third formal warning, breach procedures will be invoked. The offender is usually able to continue with Supervised Attendance activities whilst awaiting a court hearing for breach.

The Tayside Scheme

(i)   Staffing and Accommodation

1.21   The social work department holds statutory responsibility for the Order, with all organisational and delivery aspects being carried out by APEX Scotland as the Order manager. APEX is a charitable organisation whose remit is to assist offenders and those at risk of offending, to obtain employment or job training. It was considered that as APEX had extensive experience in running modular courses for offenders, that they were more qualified to organise and run the educational courses than the social work department and could perhaps encourage those on a SAO to participate in activities and to seek training or employment on completion of the Order.

1.22   The social work department staff consist of two qualified social workers and one social work assistant (plus part-time clerical support), all of whom have a SAO caseload only and report to the Principal Officer (Offenders). The social workers attend each FEC for the first few months of operation within each court, frequently assessing the offender prior to sentence when asked to do so, undertake a post-sentence interview at the SAO office and conduct a brief interview at the end of the Order (to comply with the Rehabilitation of Offenders Act 1974). The post-sentence interview includes a briefing about the SAO stressing the penalties for non-compliance and usually lasts for about 30 minutes (reduced from one hour in the early stages) which is credited to the SAO. The intention is to integrate the running of Supervised Attendance within the Offender Services team once the scheme is fully operational throughout Tayside with APEX continuing as the Order manager.

1.23   APEX staff consist of one senior trainer and an administrative support, with another officer having been appointed later to assist with Perth and Angus courts. APEX interview the offender on arrival to develop the Order Plan which commences with the 10-hour core module, presented by APEX staff. This interview lasts a further 30 minutes (previously 60 to 90 minutes) which is also credited to the SAO and includes a discussion of the offenders' fears, what they might expect to get out of the Order and a reinforcement of the rules.

1.24   The SAO social work staff have an office within the Offender Services offices of the social work department located near to the courts. APEX have large premises also in central Dundee consisting of offices, two workshops and rooms suitable for seminars and other educational activities.

(ii)   Types of Offender and Activities (Tayside)

1.25   The physically handicapped offender can be accommodated as the SAO office and the APEX premises are all on the ground floor. Sessions will be arranged, as necessary, for evenings and weekends to suit those in employment. APEX work with people with other special needs and can therefore extend this experience to offenders on a SAO.

1.26   The core module activities are referred to as the stage I module and can be viewed as 'educational activities'. This consists of four 2.5 hour sessions covering welfare rights; money management; debt counselling and employment guidance. Variations in the flow of Orders per month do not affect the provision of the core module as individual sessions are provided when necessary. Those with more than a 10-hour Order are reviewed by APEX and the SAO staff to assess the offender's needs, skills and experience and construct an Order Plan. Some offenders then progress to the stage II module which is a more in-depth examination of a core module topic for those considered to be in need of this (although only one person had undertaken a stage II module by the end of the research period). A range of stage II activities (drugs and alcohol education, and welfare rights) had been agreed with other agencies but these had not been required by the end of the fieldwork. The stage III module seems to be partly 'constructive use of time' (for example, learning computer skills and how to make toys for playgroups - both at the APEX workshop - attending a first-aid course and assisting sports officers with people with learning difficulties at a football club) and partly 'unpaid work' (for example, car washing for senior citizens supervised by private garage companies, cleaning telephone boxes and cleaning graffiti off buses).

(iii)   Supervision, Discipline and Breach (Tayside)

1.27   In the event of failure to comply at the place of work, APEX will telephone the supervising social worker in the first instance and then confirm in writing. Any absence will be followed up the same day as notification. Disciplinary action follows those set out in the guidelines (see paragraph 1.8). Failure to report to the supervising social worker at the beginning of the Order is a breach of requirement of the Order and is considered to be particularly serious.

The Highland Scheme

(i)   Staffing and Accommodation

1.28   The Highland scheme is organised and managed by the Area Team Leader (Development) Offender Services, to whom two social work staff report, each being responsible for both SAOs and Community Service, one in Inverness and the other in Invergordon (to cover the Tain and Dingwall Sheriff Courts). Existing Community Service supervisors take the offenders on a SAO to their place of work and are responsible for their supervision. The office accommodation for the SAOs are located in the Community Service offices. The SAO reporting structures and other procedures follow those of Community Service.

1.29   On being given a SAO, the offender is told in court to contact the court duty officer (social worker) who directs the offender to contact the SAO office. The responsibility to arrange the post-sentence interview (which must take place within one week of sentence) is placed on the offender rather than the SAO staff "running after the offender". This interview covers the conditions of the Order, previous convictions and an assessment of needs and commitments and lasts about 20 minutes but is not credited to the Order. The needs and views of the offender are taken into consideration before being informally matched to a placement which is usually determined by availability rather than needs.

(ii)   Types of Offender and Activities (Highland)

1.30   Offenders with special needs can be accommodated. The workshop environment is suited to those with a physical disability and the SAO budget can cover childminders for single parents. Placements can be arranged in the evening or weekend to suit those in employment or with other commitments.

1.31   The scheme is very similar to Community Service and only unpaid work is undertaken. Work placements are more or less identical to those undertaken by Community Service offenders (the same agencies are used) but are carried out on different days.   The work placements carried out, either in groups or individually, up to the end of January were:

- painting and decorating the Community Service Centre and pensioners' homes
- collecting and chopping firewood
- restoring furniture
- gardening
- one offender was on an individual placement working in a Salvation Army soup kitchen.

(iii)   Supervision, Discipline and Breach (Highland)

1.32   offenders on a SAO are supervised by the Community Service supervisors at all times when working in groups.   When an offender is in an individual placement, the agency involved will check the work periodically.   Offenders are assessed for risk and need for constant supervision, prior to allocation to placements.   SAO staff will liaise with supervisors and agencies on a weekly basis and will check on quality of work.

1.33   The policy is that SAO staff will be contacted by the supervisors or the agency immediately on an absence and SAO staff will visit the offender that day or the following morning if the placement was scheduled for an evening.   Definitions of acceptable absences and the procedures for formal warnings and breach follow those set out in the Social Work Services Group guidelines.

D.   Research Objectives and Methodology

1.34   The aims of the research are to monitor and evaluate the establishment and operation of the pilot schemes and the national guidelines, to assist the revision of the guidelines into National Standards and to inform the design of further schemes.

1.35   The research objectives are:

1. To monitor the establishment of the pilot schemes.

2. To describe the use currently made by courts in the pilot schemes of imprisonment and of alternatives to imprisonment for fine default.

3. To monitor the pilot schemes and evaluate the operational effectiveness and value of the national guidelines.

4. To evaluate the efficiency and effectiveness of the pilot schemes in terms of the objectives set out by the national guidelines.

1.36   Objective 1 - The establishment of schemes was monitored by conducting interviews prior to the start of the schemes with five sentencers and five clerks to the courts and those officers of the social work departments most concerned with the establishment of the schemes, and by extracting information from policy documents.

1.37   Objective 2 - Data contained in Fines Enquiry Court lists between 1989 and 1991 and from the start of the schemes were used to describe the use made of imprisonment and of alternatives to imprisonment for fine default both prior to and following the introduction of SAOs.   This source of data was chosen as it proved to be the only readily accessible source of data once court records were computerised and presented similar data both prior to and following computerisation.   FEC lists for 1989 were not available in Ayr.   It was decided that FEC lists would not be analysed in Perth Sheriff and District Courts (which commenced in November 1992) as it was not expected that many SAOs would have been imposed by the end of the fieldwork and that the impact on sentencing practices would be minimal.

1.38   Objectives 3 and 4 - The methods involved in monitoring and evaluating the schemes and guidelines included:

- Extracting data on all those cited to attend, from FEC lists (which provide basic data only); the complaint and attached papers for those given a SAO or a custodial sentence (which provide details on the original fine and previous convictions); and SAO records which provide data on the activities undertaken, the attendance and behaviour record and outcome of the SAO, from the start of each scheme until the 31st January 1993.

- Interviewing sentencers, clerks to the court, SAO staff and agencies providing activities at the end of the period of fieldwork (after January 1993) to obtain their views on the procedures and operation of the scheme and interviewing offenders given a SAO on completion of their Order to obtain their views on their experience of the SAO, with some further offenders being interviewed in February prior to completion of their SAO, but having completed at least 10 hours (to increase the total number of interviews, as insufficient numbers had completed their SAO by the end of January).

- A self-completion questionnaire for those sentencers, clerks and offenders who were unwilling to be interviewed or for whom it was decided that a personal interview was inappropriate.

1.39   Sentencers attached to each court in the pilot schemes were invited for interview if they had imposed more than two SAOs, to obtain their views on their experience of the SAO and views of the guidelines.   Sheriffs and justices who had imposed two or less SAOs were invited to complete a self-completion questionnaire, some of whom refused as they considered that they had insufficient experience on which to base any views.   It is, however, accepted that as only nine of the 34 sentencers who had imposed a SAO by the end of January agreed to be interviewed or to complete a self-completion questionnaire (26%), their views may not be representative of all those who had imposed a SAO. Clerks to each court and agencies supervising the activities were invited for interview or invited to complete a self-completion questionnaire if preferred.   Each of the 60 offenders who had completed their SAO by the end of February 1993 were invited for interview or, if they refused, were asked to complete a self-completion questionnaire.   Forty-one offenders who had completed their SAO were interviewed and five returned a self-completion questionnaire (77%).   In addition, a further 12 offenders who had completed at least 10 hours by March 1993 were interviewed.   The number of interviews and self-completion questionnaires conducted were:

Interviews	3 sheriffs
	1 justice
	1 sheriff clerk
	53 offenders
	13 agencies
	all SAO staff

Self-completion	3 sheriffs
Questionnaires:	2 justices
	1 sheriff clerk
	5 offenders

1.40   Interviews with sentencers, clerks to the court and SAO staff were undertaken by the research consultant, and offenders and agencies were interviewed by three local researchers employed by the research consultant.   Data were extracted from court records by the researchers and SAO staff assisted the researchers in extracting data from SAO records.

E.   Social Work Department Liaison with Courts (pre-pilot)

1.41   Part of the monitoring of the establishment of the pilot schemes covered the extent to which the social work departments liaised with the courts prior to the implementation of the schemes.   The Social Work Services Group guidelines stress the importance of local authorities gaining the co-operation of sentencers to enable the objectives of the Order to be achieved, in particular to discuss with them:

> the guidelines
>
> the range of available activities
>
> the kinds of offender for whom provision can be made
>
> the likely level of demand for SAOs

1.42   Social work managers from each of the pilot areas conducted formal meetings and also had regular informal contact with sentencers and clerks on many occasions from the initial planning stages until the commencement of the scheme in their area, to brief the courts about the development of the social work department's proposals and to invite their comments.

1.43   The researcher obtained the views of a representative sample of sentencers and the clerk to the court in all but one court covered by the pilot schemes, regarding the period prior to the commencement of schemes.   It was reported by sentencers and clerks that, at the meetings between social work managers and the courts, the social work department proposals were presented but specific discussions and negotiation about the guidelines, kinds of offender and potential level of demand did not always take place.   Feedback from the research interviews suggested that sentencers and clerks tended to view the guidelines and specific activities as matters not directly concerning themselves and that the social work managers tended to view appropriate types of offender as a matter for the sentencers.   Despite these perceptions, respondents provided some general comments on types of activities, types of offenders, the SAO leaflet and a tariff system.

(i)   Types of Activity

1.44   In the initial planning stages sentencers exerted some influence on the type of activities to be provided.   For example, the original concept of education-only activities in Tayside was changed to include some unpaid work partly to accommodate the views of some sentencers.   (At that time, APEX spoke to fine defaulters in prison to gauge how they would respond to a SAO and to different types of activities.   These defaulters indicated a preference for a combination of practical and educational activities).   Sheriffs and the social work managers in Highland favoured the Community Service approach rather than educational activities partly because they viewed a fine as a punishment and considered Community Service type work to be more of a punishment than educational activities. The view that the punitive element of the SAO is 'the fine on time' was disregarded by some in Highland as the unemployed (ie most defaulters) have plenty of time therefore attendance would not be punitive. The Highland social work department felt that if fine defaulters required an educational input, they should have been given a Probation Order in the first instance and that inability to pay did not necessarily mean inability to manage money and need for education on money management. Sentencers in all schemes tended to hold the view that the educational aspect of the SAO might be viewed as a 'soft option' by the community.

(ii)   Types of Offender

1.45   Most sentencers thought that the SAO would suit those unable to pay as opposed to unwilling to pay, the latter being more likely to receive a custodial sentence. It was suggested that other factors which might influence the sentencing decision could include the balance of the outstanding fine and whether the defaulter had started to pay it. One justice thought that the SAO would be ideal for the single parent fined for not paying the TV licence and being unable to afford to pay the fine.

(iii)   The SAO Leaflet

1.46   The main issue raised by clerks of court was the leaflet originally intended to be sent to those cited to attend a FEC to inform offenders about the SAO prior to their agreement to the order. Some clerks to the court questioned whether a leaflet should be sent with the citation as, although the offender has to agree to a Probation Order and to a Community Service Order, a leaflet describing these court disposals is not given to the offender prior to the offender's agreement. The clerk to Dundee District Court thought it would be a waste of time as offenders from that court frequently pay the outstanding fine after having received the citation. It was decided that offenders in Dundee District and Sheriff Courts should receive the leaflet when they attend the court rather than it being sent out with the citation, which is the procedure followed in the Ayr and Highland.

1.47   In two schemes, the sheriff clerks suggested changes to the leaflet, for example, to ensure that it was clear that the SAO was only one option open to sentencers at the FEC. One SAO officer suggested that SAO managers and officers could have jointly drafted the basis of the leaflet which would be common to all schemes to avoid duplication of effort and that the distinctive features of each scheme be added to their own leaflet.

(iv)   A Tariff System

1.48   The main issue raised by sentencers at meetings between the social work managers and the courts was whether a tariff system should operate which would link the SAO hours imposed to the level of outstanding fine. (One achievement of the Tayside scheme was the organisation of a joint meeting of sheriffs and justices which was well attended and resulted in a useful discussion about the scheme and in particular whether a tariff system should operate). It was felt by some sentencers in the three areas that they would use a rough tariff system in most cases with one hour being equivalent to about £5 whereas other sentencers said they would not use a tariff system but would consider each case individually.

Conclusion

1.49   It is evident that Supervised Attendance Orders are being piloted in three areas which are different in relation to: the types of activities provided; the agencies providing the activities; staffing and reporting structures; and demographic characteristics.

1.50   Research interviews conducted prior to schemes commencing identified a wide range of views on the role and potential effectiveness of the three models and identified the main issues which concerned the courts at that time (the tariff system and the leaflet for offenders).

1.51   The following chapters examine the impact of the SAO on sentencing practices, (including the use of the SAO as an alternative to imprisonment), the monitoring of the pilot schemes, an evaluation of the pilot schemes and an evaluation of the effectiveness of the guidelines.   The final chapter identifies some areas of good practice for future schemes.

2. THE IMPACT OF THE SAO ON SENTENCING PRACTICES

A. Background

2.1   An evaluation of the impact which the Supervised Attendance Order may have on sentencing practices would ideally be undertaken once the teething problems had been overcome and when a large number of Orders had been imposed. As this research was conducted during the initial stages of the pilot schemes and as fieldwork was completed at the end of January 1993, representing between only four months (Ayr) and seven months (Tain) of operation, the research results can only provide an indication of how SAOs might influence sentencing practice in the future. The research therefore focuses on the differences in sentencing practices between the courts in the pilot schemes which may assist in assessments of the feasibility of establishing SAO schemes in areas with certain traditions in sentencing practices.

2.2   This chapter examines the sentencing practices in previous years and compares it with the period of research to assess the extent to which the SAO may have had any influence. The source of data on all those fined in each court is The Scottish Office Home and Health Department unpublished Civil and Criminal Justice Statistics and the sources of data on those who defaulted are FEC lists and the details of those fine defaulters attending custody and other courts. It was decided that data would not be extracted from Perth Sheriff and District Court lists as it was not expected that many SAOs would be imposed between the commencement of the SAO in these courts (November 1992) and the end of the period of fieldwork (January 1993) and that the impact on sentencing practices would thus be minimal.

2.3   Figures throughout this report relate to cases not persons unless otherwise stated (one person can have many fines, each with a separate case reference number and possible a different disposal for each). Figures include cases which were subject to a Compensation Order in addition to a fine as such cases were not identified on court lists. The amount of fine outstanding therefore includes the amount of compensation (if any).

B. Fines and Default

2.4   The total number of persons fined decreased in Ayr, Dundee Sheriff and Dundee District Courts between 1989 and 1991 but in Highland the number increased between 1989 and 1990 then decreased in 1991 to a level similar to that of 1989. However, those fined as a proportion of all those with a charge proved (Table I) remained remarkably constant within each court between 1989 and 1991, with Dundee District Court having the highest use of the fine and Dundee Sheriff Court the lowest. The rates of use in Dundee District Court were marginally above those for Scotland.

Table I.   Those Fined as a Proportion of Those with Charge Proved

	1989	1990	1991
Scotland	77 %	77%	76%
Ayr Sheriff	68%	65%	64%
Dundee Sheriff	59%	59%	58%
Dundee District	81%	81%	77%
Highland	74%	74%	72%

2.5   The courts in the pilot areas vary to some extent in their general sentencing practices, for example, the proportion of those fined in each court who subsequently default and are cited to attend a FEC. An estimate of the level of default can be made by calculating the number of cases cited to Fines Enquiry Courts within a year (excluding repeat citations) as a proportion of all fines imposed that year. [1] Table II shows that Dundee District Court had the highest proportion of defaulters, followed by Ayr and Dundee Sheriff Courts, and lastly the Highland courts which had a very low rate of default. None showed any particular trend between 1989 and 1991.

Table II.   Rate of Default (citations as a percentage of all fines imposed)

	1989	1990	1991
Ayr Sheriff	-	41%	66%
Dundee Sheriff	46%	34%	51%
Dundee District	69%	55%	77%
Highland courts	18%	28%	28%

2.6   It is also interesting to explore the extent to which fine defaulters are representative of all those fined in respect of their general characteristics. The sex of defaulters 1989-1991 was found to be very similar to all those fined in each court, with the proportion of females being much higher in the district court (18% to 20%) than in the sheriff courts (2% to 8%). Unfortunately the age of defaulters was not regularly available between 1989 and 1991 except for Dundee Sheriff Court. A comparison of defaulters with all those fined in Dundee Sheriff Court 1989-1991 showed that a higher proportion of defaulters were aged less than 21 than all those fined and that the proportion aged 21 to 25 were almost identical in both groups (see Table III).

Table III.   Age of Defaulters and All Those Fined (Dundee Sheriff Court)

Age-group	1989 Default	1989 Fined	1990 Default	1990 Fined	1991 Default	1991 Fined
< 21	38%	26%	43%	26%	42%	24%
21 to 25	26%	25%	27%	25%	25%	24%
26 and over	35%	49%	30%	49%	33%	52%
Total no. = 100%	1237	1993	920	1672	920	1386

2.7   Table IV shows the amount of outstanding fine for each court. Dundee District Court had the greatest proportion of defaulters with fines outstanding of less than £50 compared to other courts whereas Highland tended to have higher amounts of fine outstanding than other courts.

---

[1] It is recognised that this does not allow for the fines of many of those cited in a year having been imposed in previous years. FEC lists do not provide the date of the original fine.

Table IV.   Amount of Fine Outstanding

	1989	1990	1991
Ayr Sheriff			
< £50	+	34%	29%
£50 < £100	+	34%	32%
£100 and over	+	32%	39%
Total no. = 100%*	+	859	1130
Dundee Sheriff Court			
<£50	27%	22%	23%
£50 < £100	31%	32%	31%
£100 and over	42%	47%	46%
Total no. = 100%*	1095	684	920
Dundee District Court			
< £50	80%	77%	69%
£50 < £100	16%	17%	23%
£100 and over	3%	6%	8%
Total no. = 100%*	2390	1902	2173
Highland Courts			
< £50	24%	22%	19%
£50 < £100	26%	26%	28%
£100 and over	50%	51%	53%
Total no. = 100%*	398	521	508

* Excludes those who paid prior to the FEC. Due to rounding percent. may not equal 100

+ Figures for 1989 were not available in Ayr

C.   Rate of Attendance at FECs

2.8   Another point of variation exists in the proportion of cases cited to a Fines Enquiry Court between 1989 and 1991 who did not attend.   Table V shows that the proportion of those cited where a warrant was issued for non-attendance was lowest in Dundee Sheriff Court although during the pilot, the rate for Dundee Sheriff Court increased to a level similar to, but still lower than that of other courts.   Reasons for what would appear to be high levels of non-attendance were not available in this study but could be a subject of further research.

Table V.   Warrants for Non-Attendance (as a percentage of all citations)

	1989	1990	1991	Pilot
Ayr Sheriff	*	39%	42%	44%
Dundee Sheriff	20%	18%	21%	31%
Dundee District	42%	33%	35%	36%
Highland	40%	39%	37%	35%

* Figures for 1989 were not available in Ayr

2.9   The proportion of cases cited to FECs and other courts from 1989 to 1991 who paid the outstanding fine at the Bar ranged from one per cent to eight per cent. In addition, one third of cases cited to attend Dundee District Court paid prior to the date of the court between 1989 and 1991, compared to between 10 and 21 per cent in Highland, 7 and 20 per cent in Ayr and 2 to 7 per cent in Dundee Sheriff Court. During the pilot the rate remained the same in Dundee Sheriff Court but dropped to 25 per cent in the district court, 5 per cent in Highland and only one case paid prior to the date of the court in Ayr. These reductions could perhaps be explained by the computerisation of FEC lists which provides an updated list for the court thus excluding those who had paid since the citations were served.

D.   Court Disposals

2.10   The following table shows the changes in court practices between 1989 and 1991 and the period of fieldwork which was between the summer of 1992 and the end of January 1993 and is referred to in this report as the 'pilot'. The percentages in Table VI are based on the number of fine default cases (not individuals) disposed of by the courts. The relevant court disposals are the imposition of: a) SAO; b) Custody; c) Pay by a Certain Date; d) Level of instalments changed or to be continued ('More Time to Pay'); e) Fine Remitted; and f) The Alternative, which is imposed in addition to 'Pay by Certain Date' and 'More Time to Pay'. Throughout the report the term 'The Alternative' relates to the custodial sentence imposed by the court when ordering payment of the fine by a certain date or setting a level of instalments, to be implemented if the offender defaults on these methods of payment. The offender is then admitted to custody without returning to court.

Table VI.   Disposals of Fine Defaulters by Court and Year.

	1989	1990	1991	Pilot
Supervised Attendance				
Ayr	-	-	-	15%
Dundee Sheriff	-	-	-	7%
Dundee District	-	-	-	16%
Highland	-	-	-	13%
Custodial sentence				
Ayr	*	20%	25%	9%
Dundee Sheriff	14%	17%	9%	9%
Dundee District	1%	4%	1%	4%
Highland	2%	13%	12%	8%
Pay by Certain Date				
Ayr	*	9%	14%	7%
Dundee Sheriff	4%	5%	6%	3%
Dundee District	8%	10%	10%	5%
Highland	6%	8%	11%	10%
More Time to Pay				
Ayr	*	70%	59%	68%
Dundee Sheriff	81%	78%	84%	80%
Dundee District	77%	72%	78%	73%
Highland	91%	75%	71%	69%

	1989	1990	1991	Pilot
Fine Remitted				
Ayr	*	1%	1%	2%
Dundee Sheriff	1%	1%	1%	1%
Dundee District	14%	13%	11%	1%
Highland	1%	3%	5%	0%
Total no.=100%				
Ayr	*	372	480	232
Dundee Sheriff	783	598	562	349
Dundee District	452	417	465	238
Highland	182	267	235	171
Alternative [1]				
Ayr	*	12%	45%	38%
Dundee Sheriff	54%	21%	43%	43%
Dundee District	56%	24%	44%	32%
Highland	54%	19%	49%	42%

* Figures for Ayr were not available for 1989.

(i)   Supervised Attendance

2.11   Dundee Sheriff Court had the lowest proportion of cases attending court given a SAO (7% compared to 13% in Highland, 15% in Ayr and 16% in Dundee District Court). It should be noted that this table refers to cases not individuals and that in Dundee District Court there were 29 offenders who received a SAO relating to 39 cases; in Highland 14 defaulters were given a SAO relating to 22 cases; in Ayr 34 SAOs were imposed relating to 35 cases and in Dundee Sheriff Court 23 SAOs were imposed relating to the same number of cases.

(ii)   Custody

2.12   It is important to note that the figures for custodial sentences do not relate to offenders <u>received</u> into custody for fine default as some of those given a custodial sentence may pay their fine prior to reception. The figures also exclude those who had been given more time to pay with the alternative of a custodial sentence and who subsequently defaulted and were taken directly to prison without appearing before the court. (These alternative routes into custody, or avoidance of custody, are not directly relevant to an assessment of changes in court practices, although they may be relevant to an examination of the influence of the SAO on offender behaviour in relation to admission to custody, which will be discussed in chapter 4).

2.13   It is evident that the proportion of cases receiving a custodial sentence decreased markedly in Ayr since the introduction of the SAO. The other courts did not display any trends (in Dundee Sheriff Court, the proportion remained the same as in 1992; in Dundee District Court it increased to the same level as in 1990 and in the Highland courts the proportion given a custodial sentence decreased but was still higher than the level in 1989). A higher proportion of cases dealt with in Dundee Sheriff Court received a custodial sentence than a SAO, whereas in the other courts the reverse was evident. During the pilot, a similar proportion of cases in each court were given a custodial sentence.

---

[1]The 'Alternative' is an additional disposal to 'Pay by Certain Date' or 'More Time to Pay' and is thus shown separately.

The ' alternative' is not implemented if the fine is eventually paid on time.

(iii)   Pay By Certain Date

2.14   There was a slight reduction since 1991 in all courts in the use of the order to pay the outstanding fine by a certain date during the pilot period but this resulted in a level of use only marginally lower than that of previous years (but higher in the case of Highland).

(iv)   More Time To Pay

2.15   There was some difference between courts in the proportion of defaulters given more time to pay.   For example, Highland had the highest level of 91 per cent in 1989 which decreased each year to 69 per cent during the pilot.   On the other hand, the levels in Dundee Sheriff and District Courts fluctuated over the years within a narrow range and the level in Ayr dropped in 1991 but during the pilot, returned to a similar level as 1990.

(v)   Fine Remitted

2.16   The level of remission of fines has remained at a very low level in all courts except Dundee District Court where the proportion of all defaulters dealt with in court was as high as 14 per cent in 1989 but dropped to one per cent during the pilot period.   The reasons for this change were not explored in this study but could be a subject of further research.

(vi)   The Alternative

2.17   All courts demonstrated a surprisingly similar pattern of level of use of the alternative for fine default with the exception of a rather low figure in Ayr in 1990.   This pattern showed that the alternative was imposed on over half of defaulters attending courts in 1989, dropping to less than one quarter in 1990 to rise again to between 43 per cent and 49 per cent in 1991 and decreasing during the pilot period, with the exception of Dundee Sheriff Court which remained at the same level as 1991.

2.18   One might have expected that the use of the alternative would have decreased markedly during the pilot period as sentencers might have preferred to have seen these defaulters again in court to assess whether a SAO or custody would be more suitable.   It could be argued that sentencers had made that assessment at the time of imposing the alternative and had decided that a custodial sentence would be more appropriate than a SAO should default then occur.   Feedback from SAO staff who had attended FEC courts indicated that some sentencers were imposing the alternative on offenders who were, in their view, eminently suitable for a SAO and suggested that in some cases, the sentencer had forgotten about the availability of this new court disposal. This was perhaps more evident with sentencers who had little experience of using the SAO and who perhaps did not sit frequently at courts where the SAO was available.

E.   District Courts

2.19   As Dundee was the only district court included in this part of the study, it is perhaps worthwhile to make some assessment of the extent to which it is representative of other district courts.   Those courts selected for comparison were most of the district courts in the areas where a scheme was operating in the sheriff courts (Inverness, Ross & Cromarty, Nairn, Perth & Kinross, Angus, Kyle & Carrick and Cumnock & Doon Valley District Courts).   Like Dundee, the number of fines decreased in all of these district courts between 1990 and 1991 except in Ross & Cromarty and Angus, where the number increased.   Cumnock & Doon Valley imposed much lower fines than the other district courts in the pilot areas (60% to 73% were fines of under £50 compared to 23% to 48% of fines in the other district courts between 1989 and 1991).

Dundee District Court had a lower use of the fine between 1989 and 1991 (77% to 81%) compared to other district courts (82% to 94%).

2.20   The proportion of females as a proportion of all those fined varied between district courts, with Perth & Kinross having a consistently lower rate between 1989 and 1991 (9% to 11%) than the other district courts, and the Highland courts having the highest proportion (for example, Inverness had 23% to 25%). Between 1989 and 1991 the most common age group in district courts of all those fined was males aged 26 and over who accounted for 38 to 62 per cent. Dundee District Court was about average within these ranges.   Dundee was therefore fairly typical of district courts in relation to the number and amount of fines imposed and the gender of those fined.

F.   Computerisation of Court Records

2.21   Statistics on sentencing practices may have been affected by the computerisation of court records which took place prior to the introduction of SAOs in most courts.   Records were previously trawled manually to identify fine defaulters to be cited to FECs and sometimes this occurred infrequently.   With computerisation, fine defaulters are identified immediately and FECs are held more frequently.   During computerisation, records were not trawled and FECs were delayed.   This resulted in, for example, the postponement of the December 1991 FEC in Dundee Sheriff Court which would affect numbers attending FECs in that year.   As most of the analyses are based on proportions rather than numbers and as there is no reason to believe that those who would have attended that court were any different from defaulters attending courts in previous months, it is thought that computerisation should not have had a significant effect on the conclusions on sentencing practices (although delayed trawls give defaulters more time to pay without being cited to a FEC).

Conclusion

2.22   The research findings identified marked differences between courts in some aspects of sentencing practice but similarities in others.   For example, Dundee District Court was found to be fairly typical of other district courts but it varied from the sheriff courts in some aspects.   It had:

> the highest use of the fine
>
> the highest rate of defaulters
>
> the highest proportion of female defaulters
>
> the highest proportion of fines imposed and amount outstanding under £50
>
> the highest proportion of citations where the fine was paid prior to the court
>
> the highest proportion of fines remitted (prior to the pilot)
>
> the least frequent use of the custodial sentence for default

2.23   The main features of Dundee Sheriff Court were that it had:

> the lowest use of the fine
>
> the lowest rate of warrants issued for non-attendance between 1989 and 1991
>
> the lowest rate of default cases dealt with in court who were given a SAO (and was the only court which imposed a greater number of custodial sentences tha SAOs)

the lowest rate of defaulters paying their outstanding fine before the date of the court between 1989 and 1991

the lowest rate of those ordered to pay by a certain date

the highest rate of those given more time to pay

2.24   The main features of Ayr Sheriff Court were that:

it had the highest rate of warrants issued for non-attendance

it had slightly lower rates of imposition of more time to pay than other courts

it had the highest rate of defaulters given custodial sentences during 1990 and 1991

following the introduction of the SAO the proportion receiving a custodial sentence decreased markedly

2.25   Highland (consisting of Inverness, Tain and Dingwall Sheriff Courts) had only one feature which distinguished it from the other courts in relation to sentencing practices. It had the lowest default rate.

2.26   There were similarities between courts in relation to:

the proportion of all those fined whose outstanding fine was less than £50 (6% to13%) with the exception of Dundee District Court

the proportion of those cited who were issued with a warrant for non-attendance during the pilot with the exception of Ayr

the proportion of cases cited who paid the outstanding fine at the Bar (1% to 8%)

the proportion of default cases dealt with in court who were given a custodial sentence during the pilot (4% to 9%)

the proportion of cases whose fine was remitted (1% to 5%) with the exception of Dundee District Court between 1989 and 1991

2.27   This chapter has identified many differences and similarities between courts in relation to sentencing practices which allows the evaluation of the Supervised Attendance Order to be placed in context. It would appear from the data presented in this chapter that the SAO is being used as an alternative to custodial sentences in Ayr Sheriff Court, although the reduction in the use of the custodial sentence may be caused by some other factor not identified by the research. Further quantitative and qualitative data of assessments on whether the SAO is being used as an alternative to custody are provided later in the report.

2.28   It must be emphasised that because the research was undertaken during the initial phase of this new court disposal, covered a short period of operation (between four and seven months) and because the number of SAOs imposed was relatively low, firm conclusions about the long-term impact of the SAO on sentencing practices cannot be made. This would require more exhaustive and detailed research at a later date. This study, however, does provide a useful description of the 'before' stage in relation to sentencing practices and of the immediate effects of the introduction of the Supervised Attendance Order.

3. MONITORING OF THE PILOT SCHEMES

3.1   This section describes the characteristics of those given a SAO[1] and the procedures and practices of the pilot SAO schemes from their commencement until the end of January 1993 and provides the basis for the following chapter on evaluation of the efficiency and effectiveness of the schemes.

A.   Number of Hours and Tariff

3.2   The following table presents the number and hours of the SAOs imposed between the start of each scheme and the end of January 1993.

Table VII.   Number of SAO Hours by Court

	Ayr Sheriff	Dundee Sheriff	Dundee District	Highland Sheriff	Perth Both*	Total
10 hours	1	7	3	1	1	13
20 hours	4	9	8	6	1	28
30 hours	13	3	6	2	1	25
40 hours	6	1	4	2	1	14
50 hours	1	1	2	0	1	5
60 hours	9	2	6	3	2	22
Total	34	23	29	14	7	107

   * Both the sheriff and district courts

3.3   The most common length of order was the 20 hour order (26% of all orders) followed by 30 hours (23%) and 60 hours (21%).   Only five offenders were given a 50 hour order.   The most frequent length of order in Ayr was 30 hours whereas in the Dundee courts and Highland it was 20 hours and in Perth 60 hours.

3.4   Prior to the commencement of schemes, there was some discussion amongst sentencers as to whether a tariff system should operate and what it should be. After the period of research fieldwork, the sentencers in Dundee said that they operated a rough tariff of £5 per hour. A Highland sentencer said that he operated a tariff of about £3 or £4 per hour. The exception was in Ayr where sentencers said that they did not operate a tariff (although they did say that they would tend to give more hours for a large balance of fine or a serious offence). The figures for Ayr seemed to support the view that a tariff system was not in operation as 29 per cent of those with a balance of £100 or less were given 40 hours or more (but all those with a balance of over £100 received 40 hours or more). To assess whether a rough tariff system was in operation in the other courts, a comparison of the outstanding fine and the number of hours imposed was made (see Table VIII). The results showed that a crude tariff system seemed to be operating with the lower balance of fines attracting lower SAO hours. The tariff seemed to be about one hour of Supervised Attendance for each £5 of outstanding fine.

---

[1]Referred to throughout the report as 'SAO offenders'

Table VIII.   Balance of Fine by SAO Hours (all courts except Ayr)

	Up to £100	£101 - £200	£201 or over
10 hours	12	-	-
20 hours	20	4	1
30 hours	3	6	3
40 hours	1	3	3
50 hours	-	2	2
60 hours	-	-	13
Total	36	15	22

3.5   Although the schemes officially started on different dates (see paragraph 1.10), Dundee Sheriff and District Courts and Inverness Sheriff Court imposed their first SAOs in August (one SAO had been imposed in Tain in June). Ayr was about six weeks later in starting (22 September) and Perth Sheriff and District Courts did not start until November. Table IX shows that, as one would expect, the Perth courts had a low completion rate of hours and Orders by the end of the research fieldwork (end of January 1993). Ayr had the highest proportion of hours completed and the highest proportion of SAOs completed by the end of January 1993. This could cause problems in maintaining sufficient numbers in group activities in the future.

Table IX.   Completion of SA Hours and SA Orders

	Ayr	Dundee S.	Dundee D.	Highland	Perth
Total hours imposed	1280	550	970	450	270
Total hours completed	940	299	296	286	64
% hours completed	73%	54%	31%	64%	24%
No. SAOs imposed	34	23	29	14	7
No. SAOs completed	23	9	8	5	0
% SAOs completed	68%	39%	28%	36%	0%

B.   Characteristics of Defaulters

3.6   The characteristics of offenders on a SAO are compared with those of defaulters given a custodial sentence and with all defaulters attending court within the research period (referred to as "all attenders" in this report). Details about offenders on a SAO were available from social work records and the complaint. The complaint was the only source of data (in addition to the court lists) on those given a custodial sentence, but unfortunately it was not readily available in Dundee Sheriff Court, thus comparisons between these two groups of offenders from that court are limited. Data on defaulters attending courts were restricted to the court lists. As only five SAOs were imposed in Perth Sheriff Court and two in the District Court, comparisons of proportions would not be meaningful and thus these courts have been excluded from this section.

22

3.7   A greater proportion of offenders on a SAO within each court were female (21% to 30%) than those given a custodial sentence (5% to 17%) or all those attending court (7% to 16%) with the exception of Dundee Sheriff Court, where approximately 8 per cent of offenders on a SAO, those given a custodial sentence and all attenders were female.

3.8   The age of offenders on a SAO, those given a custodial sentence and all attenders varied, with a tendency in all courts for offenders on a SAO to be younger (under 21) than those given custody and all attenders (see Table X).   A greater proportion of offenders on a SAO in Dundee Sheriff Court and Highland were under 21 compared to Dundee District Court and Ayr.

Table X.   Age of those given SAO and Custody and All Attenders

	Under 21	21 - 25	26 & over	Total no.*=100%
Ayr SAO	29%	39%	33%	34
Ayr Custody	5%	32%	63%	20
Ayr Attenders	20%	33%	47%	231
Dundee S. SAO	57%	22%	22%	23
Dundee S. Custody	26%	30%	45%	27
Dundee S. Attenders	30%	33%	37%	341
Dundee D. SAO	38%	41%	20%	29
Dundee D. Custody	-	50%	50%	6
Dundee D. Attenders	17%	35%	47%	163
Highland SAO	57%	21%	21%	14
Highland Custody	33%	33%	33%	12
Highland Attenders	41%	22%	36%	126

* Total for the row and excludes those where age was not available. Due to rounding, percentages may not equal 100.

3.9   Data relating to the marital status and employment status of defaulters given a custodial sentence and that of all attenders were not regularly available but were available for offenders on a SAO. A higher proportion of offenders on a SAO in Dundee Sheriff and District Courts were single (74% and 69%) compared to other courts (54% and 48%) and between 71 and 79 per cent were unemployed in all courts.

3.10   There was no evidence of any similarities between courts in the amount of fine outstanding by offenders on a SAO, those given a custodial sentence and all attenders. In Ayr and Highland, a higher proportion of offenders on a SAO had less than £50 of fine outstanding than those given a custodial sentence and all attenders, whereas in Dundee Sheriff Court a greater proportion of those given a custodial sentence had £50 or less to pay. Contrary to what might be expected, the proportion of those given a custodial sentence with a fine outstanding of over £200 was not always greater than that of offenders on a SAO (for example in Ayr 15% of those given custody had over £200 to pay compared to 20% of offenders on a SAO).

3.11   Data on previous sentences were extracted from the complaint for those given custody and offenders on a SAO. However, the data for those given custody were not available in a sufficient number of cases in Highland and the Dundee Courts to allow comparisons to be made with offenders on a SAO but data were available in Ayr and are described in Diagram I. In Ayr a higher proportion of those given custody had experience of YOI or Prison than offenders on a SAO (44% compared to 27%).

23

Diagram I.   Previous Sentences of SAO and Custody Offenders, Ayr (percentages)

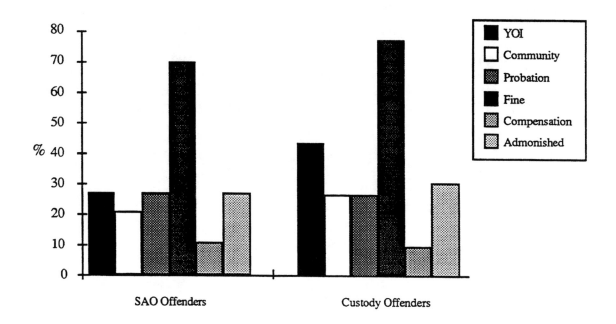

3.12   Table XI shows the number of offenders on a SAO who had previous experience of each type of sentence.   The source of data is the complaint.

Table XI.   Previous Sentences of SAO Offenders

	Ayr Sheriff	Dundee Sheriff	Dundee District	Highland Sheriff	Total %`
YOI	4	3	0	2	9%
Prison	8	5	8	3	25%
Community Service	7	9	8	4	29%
Probation	9	9	7	5	32%
Fine	24	14	19	9	69%
Compensation	4	2	2	1	9%
Admonished	9	2	3	3	18%
None	3	3	4	1	48%
Total* (known cases)#	34	20	29	12	100%

* One offender can appear in more than one category, therefore the sum of the numbers in each category does not equal the total offenders on a SAO from that court.

excludes those cases where data on previous sentences were not available.

24

3.13   Over two thirds of all offenders on a SAO had been fined before and a relatively high proportion had experience of either Prison, Community Service or Probation.   A higher proportion of offenders on a SAO from Dundee Sheriff Court had experience of Community Service compared to other courts and a greater proportion of offenders on a SAO from both Dundee Sheriff Court and Highland had experience of probation than Dundee District and Ayr. (Of the 58 offenders on a SAO who were interviewed over one half reported that they had been in YOI, prison or on remand and one quarter had served a custodial sentence for non-payment of a previous fine).   The most common groups of offences resulting in the original fine for both offenders on a SAO and those given custody on default were Motor Vehicle, Dishonesty and Breach of the Peace.

C.   Court Procedures and Practice

(i)   <u>Number of SAOs</u>

3.14   Table XII provides the number of SAOs imposed in each court and expresses that number as a rate of all fine defaulters (people as opposed to cases) attending both Fines Enquiry and other courts [1]. The figures in Table XII are based on the number of fine defaulters attending court, excluding those who paid at the Bar. In the remainder of the report "attenders" relates to those attending courts who were dealt with at that court but excluding those whose case was continued to another date and those who paid at the Bar.

Table XII.   Number of SAOs as a Rate Per 100 Attenders

	SAO no.	Rate
Ayr Sheriff	34	15.4
Dundee Sheriff	23	6.5
Dundee District	29	14.4
Highland Sheriff	14	8.7
Perth Sheriff	5	6.6
Perth District	2	11.1

3.15   The number of SAOs imposed in each court differs markedly but not necessarily in relation to the number of months in operation nor to the number of defaulters attending each court.   Although the numbers of SAOs made in Highland (Inverness, Dingwall and Tain Courts) and Perth District Courts are small, the rates per 100 fine defaulters attending courts are higher than Dundee Sheriff (which had a high number of SAOs) and Perth Sheriff Courts.   The rate ranged from 6.5 per 100 attenders in Dundee Sheriff Court to 15.4 in Ayr Sheriff Court.   As the aim of SAOs is to provide an alternative to custody for fine defaulters, it is surprising that Dundee District Court had such a high rate of Orders, as only 1 to 4 per cent of fine defaulters received a custodial sentence in Dundee District Court between 1989 and 1991 compared to 9 to 25 per cent in other courts.   These figures might suggest that the SAO was not always being used as an alternative to a custodial sentence in this court.

3.16   A few defaulters were offered the SAO in Ayr but refused (the number of refusals is not known).   Reasons given included that custody would be easier to cope with as the SAO was not

---

[1]When a warrant has been issued for non-attendance at a FEC, the defaulter can be brought before a custody court.

Some cases are continued to another day and are heard at a non-FEC court.

an easy option. Approximately eight defaulters refused the SAO in Dundee mainly because custody would be quicker than serving, for example, a 40 hour Order.   It was unknown how many had refused SAOs in Highland.

3.17   The number of defaulters given a SAO was considerably less than expected. Estimates of demand devised by social work managers were based on a proportion of receptions of defaulters into prison over the preceding year (between 50% and 80%) and the number required to make the scheme economically viable.   These estimates do not appear to have taken into account the slow start-up rate to be expected with new court disposals and would appear to be targets required for the financial viability of the scheme rather than an estimate of the possible orders which might be made within the first year of each scheme.   One factor which contributed to the gap between estimates and SAOs imposed was that the estimates covered some district courts which did not implement the SAO in the initial stages.

3.18   Table XIII shows the number of Orders imposed since SAO was made available at each court.   Although the Dundee courts officially started on 14th July, the first FEC was in August and this has been used as the start of the scheme in this table.   In Highland SAOs were available in Tain and Dingwall in late June when one SAO was imposed in Tain, but as the SAO was not available in Inverness until August and as no further SAOs were made in the other courts over the summer recess, August has been used as the start of the Highland scheme in the following table.   The 'Estimate' relates to the estimated number of SAOs which might have been imposed during the number of months of operation of the SAO within that court.

Table XIII.   Number of Orders Since Start of Each Scheme

	Ayr Sheriff	Dundee Sheriff	Dundee District	Highland Sheriff	Perth Both*
Month 1	9	5	4	7	3
Month 2	10	2	3	3	3
Month 3	9	5	3	3	1
Month 4	4	3	6	0	-
Month 5	2	6	8	0	-
Month 6	-	2	5	1	-
Total	34	23	29	14	7
Estimate	50	78	72	33	18
Total as % of Estimate	68%	29%	40%	42%	39%

* Both the sheriff and district courts.

3.19   It is evident that there was not a common pattern in the imposition of SAOs during the period of the research.   Ayr had a steady flow of orders from month one but this dropped dramatically in months four and five (January).   The pattern at Dundee Sheriff Court was erratic and numbers did not increase with time as expected.   In Dundee District Court, numbers did eventually increase from month four, but in Highland, the numbers decreased over the last few months.   An analysis of the number of SAOs imposed as a rate per 100 defaulters attending each court per month showed a wide variation within each court (Ayr - 6 to 26; Dundee Sheriff - 3 to 12; Dundee District - 5 to 42; Highland - 4 to 32; Perth - 4 to 19).   Ayr's estimate of demand was more accurate (68%) than those for the other courts (29% to 42%).   These figures suggest that new SAO schemes can perhaps expect to achieve about 40 per cent of their estimated number of SAOs during the initial stages of operation.

3.20   Further data have been obtained since the end of the research fieldwork to provide figures on the first year of each scheme.   These figures include the courts in the three pilot schemes where SAO was not available until after the main period of research :

Table XIV.   Number of SAOs in the First Year

	Number	Estimate	Rate
South Ayrshire	99	120	83%
Tayside	156	300	52%
Highland	33	60	55%
Total	288	480	60%

3.21   The proportion of achievement of estimated demand ranged from 52 per cent in Tayside to 83 per cent in South Ayrshire.   Overall a 60 per cent rate was achieved.   As the SAO was not available in all courts for the full year (many district courts commenced over six months after the sheriff courts), it cannot be expected that the number of Orders imposed would match the estimate. As estimates were partly based on varying proportions of the number of defaulters admitted to custody, it is interesting to note the extent to which these expectations were realised: Ayr estimated 83 per cent of the 144 received into custody in 1991 and achieved 69 per cent; Tayside estimated 50 per cent (during the first year and increasing thereafter) of the 600 received into custody in 1991 and achieved 26 per cent; and Highland estimated 67 per cent of approximately 90 defaulters admitted to custody in 1991 and achieved 37 per cent.

3.22   An analysis of the sentencer who imposed the SAO shows that in Ayr and Dundee Sheriff Courts one sentencer in each accounted for just under half of all SAOs, with another sentencer in each court accounting for one quarter and one third respectively.   In Dundee District Court, one justice accounted for about a quarter of SAOs and a further nine justices accounted for between 3 per cent and 17 per cent each.   In Highland the six sheriffs imposed between one and four SAOs each.   By the end of January, a total of eight sentencers had imposed a SAO at Ayr, seven at Dundee Sheriff, six in Highland, ten at Dundee District Court and 3 at the Perth courts. A total of 31 sentencers had imposed at least one SAO each, approximately one third of these were visiting sentencers. It is evident that a large number of sentencers were in a position to impose a SAO at each court but many had not used this court disposal.   SAO staff in all schemes reported their frustration when attending a FEC when potential offenders on a SAO were not being considered, because the sentencer had possibly not been fully informed of the SAO or, in their view, seemed to have forgotten about this disposal.

3.23   SAO staff at Dundee realised that sentencers frequently required to be reminded about the SAO and that it was also important to ensure that solicitors were briefed and reminded about this new disposal.   Although the number of SAOs imposed at the courts in Dundee was not high, the SAO staff felt that their presence in the courts and in the court buildings helped to ensure a steady flow of Orders.   The SAO staff also designed a leaflet for sentencers and solicitors to inform them of the SAO.   SAO staff in Highland suggested that some sentencers were not aware of the SAO or had forgotten about it (no orders were imposed in November and December and only one in January, compared to six in August).

3.24   Most of the sentencers interviewed considered that they could not have imposed more SAOs.   One sheriff felt that in his court, those who were suitable for a SAO got it.   Two justices thought that the recent reduction in attendance at FECs may have contributed to the low numbers of Orders made (numbers attending were lower in January for Dundee District and Sheriff Courts and Ayr, but data were not collected after January and numbers may have remained low between January and March when sentencers were interviewed). The number of defaulters attending court was erratic over the research period with a peak in August for Dundee sheriff (69) and Dundee District (59) Courts and in October for Ayr (61) and Highland (67). The months with the lowest attendances were July in Highland (4), September and January in Ayr (34 and 35 respectively) and January in Dundee Sheriff (29) and District (12) Courts. The average number of defaulters attending a FEC or other court per month was: Dundee Sheriff - 50; Ayr - 46; Dundee District - 34; Highland courts - 21 (Inverness, Tain and Dingwall Sheriff Courts).

(ii) The Leaflet for Offenders

3.25   In relation to the level of awareness of offenders, all offenders should have received a leaflet about SAOs prior to agreeing to undertake the Order. In Dundee, offenders did not receive the leaflet until they arrived at the court and the SAO staff suggested that attendance at FECs might have increased had offenders received the leaflet with their citation. Of the 58 offenders on a SAO who were interviewed, 61 per cent had read the leaflet, 18 per cent had received it but did not read it and a further 20 per cent said that they had not received a leaflet. Only two offenders said that they did not understand what would happen to them if they did not comply with the conditions of the order.

(iii) Pre-sentence Assessment

3.26   In Ayr and the Dundee courts SAO staff attended most FECs and were therefore available to provide a pre-sentence assessment if requested by the sentencer (although the Social Work Services Group Guidelines discouraged any pre-sentence assessment). It was intended that the attendance of SAO staff at the Dundee courts would terminate after a few months. It was suggested that some sentencers might be reluctant to make SAOs when the SAO staff were no longer there to undertake this assessment although it was hoped that sentencers would have gained sufficient confidence by then to impose SAOs without such an assessment. Overall, three sentencers did not view the lack of pre-sentence assessment as a problem but three others found it difficult to sentence if they did not have a Social Enquiry Report, Means Enquiry Report or other information about a person's circumstances.

iv) Timescales

3.27   There had been some concern that sentencers might fine some offenders knowing that they could not repay the fine, in order to give the offender a SAO on default because it is not available as a first disposal. An analysis of the interval between the date the last fine was imposed and the date of the custodial sentence or SAO provides a broad indication of whether sentencers had given defaulters the opportunity of more time to pay before discharging the fine. One could perhaps conclude that more time to pay had not previously been given to those with an interval of three months or less between the date of the imposition of the fine and the date of sentence for default. (It could take about three months to identify someone who had defaulted on their first instalment or date to pay in full and date of court appearance, and the time taken to repeat that process). Forty-two per cent given a SAO in Ayr had an interval of three months or less compared to 17 per cent in Dundee Sheriff, 8 per cent in Highland and 4 per cent in Dundee District. Between 1989 and the pilot study Ayr had the lowest proportion of attenders at court for default who were given more time to pay (an average of 66% compared to between 75% and 81% in other courts). These figures do not, of course, necessarily support the hypothesis that sentencers might be fining offenders to provide the opportunity of imposing a SAO on default but the figures suggest that it might be occurring in a few instances. More detailed research is required to enable this hypothesis to be tested.

3.28   At the other extreme, for a few offenders on a SAO the interval between the date of the fine and date of SAO was over eighteen months (6% in Ayr, 8% in Highland, 17% in Dundee Sheriff and 20% in Dundee District Courts). (Only two offenders given custody had an interval of over eighteen months and both were in Highland). It is recognised that a long interval may indicate that the offender had been paying the instalments regularly before eventually defaulting. However, two sentencers stated their belief that a fine should be set at a level which would allow the offender to repay it within twelve months.   These sentencers noted that occasionally offenders appear in their courts with fines imposed in England which would take them years to pay.

(vii)   Sentencing Criteria

3.29   Sentencers were asked to indicate those factors which influenced their decision to impose a SAO, custody or more time to pay. For the SAO, the main factor provided by sentencers was "inability to pay" .   This is borne out by the fact that all but four of the 58 offenders on a SAO who were interviewed gave "inability to pay" as their reason for not paying their fine - the others providing reasons such as "I forgot", "too much hassle" or "I was holding off". The nature of the offence, whether the explanation for default was reasonable and genuine, and the character of the offender were also mentioned by sentencers. Examples given by sentencers of types of offender suitable for SAO included a young mother or single parent who was struggling financially, the unemployed (especially 16-18 year olds) and those on benefit.

3.30   Those who can pay but are unwilling to pay were identified by sentencers as likely to receive a custodial sentence. Other factors which were identified by sentencers as possibly leading to a custodial sentence were: those with a record especially of serious offences and someone with a high balance of fine outstanding but unable to pay.   Examples of the circumstances of those likely to be given more time to pay included: those who had a good reason for not paying, if the defaulter could pay and is either needing 'a kick' or is willing to pay and one sheriff suggested that someone who was 'playing the system' would be given more time and an alternative. SAO staff were asked if the sentencer indicated in court why each offender was given a SAO. Only fifteen sentencers did, half of whom gave the reason of 'it's a last chance'.

3.31   Sentencers were asked to assess what proportion of offenders on whom they had imposed a SAO might have received a custodial sentence prior to the introduction of the SAO. (As the interviews were conducted about six weeks after the end of data collection it is not known how many SAOs each sentencer had imposed). One sentencer thought that both of the SAOs he had imposed were as an alternative to custody; two sentencers estimated half of their SAOs could have received a custodial sentence; one said 10 per cent and questioned whether it was intended as an alternative to custody; one thought none and a further two sentencers considered that the SAO was more of an alternative to more time to pay than to a custodial sentence but would give a custodial sentence if further default occurred.   However, most of those interviewed said that the aim of the SAO was to provide an alternative to custody for fine defaulters, four of whom stressed for those unable to pay their fine. (One sentencer added a secondary aim of rehabilitation and another of retribution). One sentencer reported that he would usually give a defaulter more time to pay with 'the alternative of custody' on further default but would not know how many of these offenders defaulted and were received into custody (he said he was worried about some of these people "slipping through the net"). Several sentencers stated that, prior to the availability of the SAO, they only used custody as a last resort and they thought that many of those given a custodial sentence paid their fine before being received into custody.   One sheriff in Highland said that he rarely used a custodial sentence as many defaulters only paid their fine when the police arrived on their doorstep with a warrant for their arrest.

3.32   SAO staff in Ayr felt that all offenders on a SAO would have qualified for a custodial sentence but did not know whether they would have got it.   In Highland SAO staff thought that a third might have received a custodial sentence and in Dundee estimates varied between 50 and 80 per cent.   The SAO records showed that, of the 72 cases where the SAO staff indicated the disposal which the offender might have received prior to the availability of the SAO, 76 per cent said custody, 6 per cent more time to pay and 18 per cent an alternative imposed.   SAO staff thought that the majority of offenders on a SAO were suitable for the SAO, the main reasons being: unable to pay the fine, unemployed and facing a custodial sentence. Although SAO staff found it very difficult to assess what type of disposal the offenders on a SAO might have received prior to this disposal being made available, it would appear that they tended to be more optimistic in its use as an alternative to custody.

3.33   Offenders were asked what sentence they thought they would have received at their last FEC when their SAO was awarded: 13 per cent said a SAO; 38 per cent custody; 36 per cent more time to pay; 11 per cent instalments reduced and 2 per cent gave other responses. Thus nearly half of those interviewed thought that they would be given another chance to pay their fine.   When asked why they thought they had been given a SAO, two said that they had asked the sentencer to consider that disposal.   Other reasons given included "I couldn't afford to pay the fine"; "because of my child"; "the court wanted to try out this new scheme"; "the jails are overcrowded and it costs less"; and "it's a greater punishment than prison because it takes longer".

D.   The SAO Procedures and Practices

(i)   The Size of Groups

3.34   In the Ayr scheme, the flow of orders affected the viability of one agency activity on assertiveness training which they felt could only work if there were a sufficient number of people who were motivated and could all go through the course together, as group cohesion was important.   It was agreed to postpone this group until numbers increased.   The focus of some presentations was changed to adapt to the circumstances of those attending, for example, single parents would have different needs in relation to safety instruction than young single men. Presentation methods have developed, for example one agency changed from a lecture presentation to a more participatory approach, as a direct result of feedback from the offenders who are asked to evaluate each session.   Both Ayr and Dundee have developed a flexible approach to improve the activities offered and to adapt to the circumstances of offenders.

3.35   The size of groups varied between one and twenty offenders dependent on the flow of orders.   Ayr did not provide educational activities for individuals, which resulted in the suspension of operating the core module prior to other activity modules.   APEX (covering the Dundee and Perth courts), on the other hand, did provide one-to-one sessions on the core module when necessary but it was suggested that this could be seen as an inefficient use of resources, especially when the scheme was extended to other areas within the region.   The APEX manager did not consider 20 to be too large a group as it could promote better discussion than when only one or two people are present.   Large groups did not hinder the participation and workshop methods they adopted.

3.36   The majority (64%) of offenders who were interviewed thought that the size of groups they had participated in were about right, although 20 per cent considered there to be too few members (groups of between 1 and 6) and 11 per cent considered there to be too many (in groups of 3 or more).   Comments provided by respondents ranged from those who got embarrassed in front of a lot of people and preferred small groups to those who enjoyed the company of groups of 6 or more as they could make friends and get a good discussion going. One offender found the group of 20 too crowded. Seventeen per cent of those interviewed were in groups of ten or more.

(ii) Length and Timing of Sessions

3.37 Half of those offenders who did 2.5 SAO hours per week thought that was about right as, for example, it allowed them time to do other things, whereas half felt that 2.5 was too few hours and that they could do more as they were unemployed, or that they felt the Order took too long. One fifth of those doing five hours a week felt that it was not enough but the majority felt that it was about right as it fitted in with other commitments. All those with seven hours to do per week and the one with ten hours thought that level was satisfactory but the one offender interviewed who did nine hours a week thought it was too many. Overall, 69 per cent of those interviewed considered that the number of hours they did per week was about right.

3.38 The two offenders who experienced travel problems were both from Girvan and had to travel one hour each way to Ayr and their excess travel time was credited to their SAO hours. (The guidelines state that travel time in excess of one hour should be credited). Arrangements have now been made to provide activities in Girvan. Only four offenders mentioned difficulties in the timing of activities which included: 'too early in the day' and not being able to get a good bus connection so had to wait a long time at the pickup point. Half of those interviewed took public transport to attend activities, a quarter took private transport, one sixth walked and one tenth were taken by SAO transport.

(iii) Non-compliance

3.39 Table XV shows the number of unacceptable absences in each scheme up to the end of January. Comparisons between schemes are difficult as each started at different times, but a rate of unacceptable absences per completed hour provides a basis for comparison. The SWSG Guidelines suggest that any absence other than the following should be regarded as unacceptable:
- certificated ill health
- in custody
- prior approval by the supervising officer
- unforeseen requirements placed on an individual by his/her employer
- when offender is faced with an unforeseen crisis arising from other responsibilities

Table XV.   Unacceptable Absences

Absences

	Ayr Sheriff	Dundee Sheriff	Dundee District	Highland Sheriff	Perth Both*
One	9	6	4	1	0
Two	3	5	5	1	3
Three	0	3	1	1	2
Four or more	3	0	0	1	1
Total offenders	15	14	10	4	6
Total Unacceptable Absences	32	25	17	10	17
Completed Hours:	940	299	296	286	64
Rate per 100 completed hours:	3	8	6	3	27

  * Both the sheriff and district court.

3.40   Perth had by far the highest rate of unacceptable absences per 100 completed SAO hours (27), followed by Dundee Sheriff and District Courts.   The main reasons given for absences classified as unacceptable were: no reason given; uncertificated illness; slept-in; and (unspecified) family problems considered by the SAO staff to be unacceptable.   During the period of research, seven offenders in each of Ayr, Dundee Sheriff and Dundee District courts had no absences compared to five in Highland and two in Perth.

3.41   Only one offender had been breached by the end of January.   He was in the Highland scheme, had a 10-hour order, was given considerable support by SAO staff to complete his hours but failed and was given a 40-hour order on breach.   Two applications had been made to Dundee Sheriff Court for breach (39 hours completed out of a 60-hour order and a 10-hour order which had not been started) and in Ayr, the Perth Courts and Dundee District Court, one application had been made to each court for breach but none of these had been heard by the end of the fieldwork.   All applications for breach related to non-attendance (three offenders had five unacceptable absences, two had three and the remaining two had disappeared).   One of those with five absences had also attended the activity late on four occasions.   An application for breach was not necessarily made after three unacceptable absences and delayed breach tactics were sometimes used for some of these offenders who were, by the end of the research period, continuing to comply with their Order but in one case, the SAO staff were considering invoking breach procedures.

Conclusion

3.42   The following are the main issues arising from the monitoring of the pilot schemes:

1.   Characteristics of offenders on a SAO.

- Females in all courts except Dundee Sheriff Court, were over-represented amongst offenders on a SAO compared to those receiving a custodial sentence and all attenders.

- Those aged under 21 were over-represented amongst offenders on a SAO in all courts.

- About three-quarters of all offenders on a SAO were unemployed.

- Over one quarter of all offenders on a SAO had previous experience of a custodial sentence and over two-thirds of all offenders on a SAO had been fined before.

2.   Numbers of SAOs.

- Numbers of SAOs were lower than expected in each scheme (43% overall in the early stages) but showed a slight improvement in later months (60% overall throughout the first 12 months of operation).

- The importance of constantly reminding all sentencers, especially visiting sentencers, and solicitors of the existence of the SAO was stressed.

- The problem of identifying realistic estimates during the first year was noted. Those establishing new schemes in the future should take into account the inevitable slow start-up rate of new initiatives, especially when deciding upon the level of resources required in the early stages.

- Ayr and Dundee District Court had the highest rate of SAOs imposed per 100 defaulters attending court (over twice that of Dundee and Perth Sheriff Courts).

- The most common lengths of Order were 20 hours, 30 hours and 60 hours with evidence in most courts of a tariff of about one SA hour per £5 of fine outstanding.

- Ayr had the highest proportion of hours completed and the highest proportion of SAOs completed by the end of January 1993.

3. Court Procedures.

- Both Dundee and Ayr provided regular SAO staff attendance at FECs and undertook a pre-sentence assessment on potential offenders on a SAO if requested by sentencers who welcomed the additional information which this provided. It was always intended that this service be withdrawn after the initial period in Dundee and there were concerns about dependency on SAO staff for assessment.

- Sentencers tended to view those unable to pay as suitable for a SAO, those able but unwilling to pay suitable for custody and those who had a good reason for not paying, suitable for more time to pay.

- There was some evidence to suggest that almost half of those given a SAO in one court (compared to between 4% and 17% in other courts) had not been given the opportunity of more time to pay, as their SAO had been imposed within three months of the original fine. This might be seen as evidence to support the sentencers' views above, but one could suggest that if the offender was unable to pay and his/her circumstances had not altered within those three months, the fine might have been imposed in the first place because of a lack of suitable alternatives or to allow the sentencer to impose a SAO on default.

- Sentencers varied in their estimate of the proportion of those to whom they had given a SAO who might have received a custodial sentence prior to SAOs from none to 100%, despite recognising that the aim of the Order was to provide an alternative to custody for fine defaulters. SAO staff estimated that 76% of all offenders might have previously received a custodial sentence.

4. SAO Activities.

A flexible approach has been adopted by Ayr and Dundee, for example, Ayr was forced to postpone its compulsory core 10-hour module at the beginning of each Order due to lack of numbers although most offenders did undertake most of these core modules at some time during their Order. Each scheme obtained feedback from offenders on a SAO which assisted in amending the focus and presentation of some sessions. The majority of offenders thought that the size of groups (between 2 and 20) and number of hours they did per week (2.5 to 10) were about right, although some preferred shorter hours per week to allow them to continue with other commitments or leisure pursuits whereas others preferred longer hours per week so that the Order could be completed more quickly.

5. Non-compliance

Perth had the highest rate of unacceptable absences per 100 completed SAO hours (27 compared to between 3 and 8 in other courts). Only one case had been breached by the end of January (Highland). Two applications for breach had been made at Dundee Sheriff court (but the offenders had disappeared) and in Ayr, Perth and Dundee District Court one application had been made for breach but had not been heard by the end of January.

4. EVALUATION OF THE PILOT SCHEMES

4.1 One of the research objectives was to evaluate the efficiency and effectiveness of the pilot schemes in terms of the objectives set out by the national guidelines. These objectives are:

1. To provide Scottish courts with a credible community based penalty which may be used as an alternative to prison or detention for offenders who default in the payment of a fine.

2. To provide offenders in default of payment of a fine an opportunity to receive a community based penalty instead of serving a period of imprisonment or detention.

3. To ensure SAOs are characterised by the following features:

   a) the imposition of discipline on the offender through the requirement to attend his/her placement on a regular basis, to attend punctually, to behave satisfactorily during the period of attendance, and to undertake and participate in the defined activity in a proper fashion.

   b) firm and reliable supervision including the expeditious institution of breach proceedings in the event of an offender failing to comply with the terms of the order.

   c) constructive activity for offenders to undertake and participate in as part of their order.

4.2 In addition, the guidelines also set out 'operational objectives' which are:

1. To ensure that SAOs are organised and managed as an integral part of social work services provided by local authorities in relation to the criminal justice system.

2. To ensure that a sufficient number and range of activity opportunities are provided to meet the expected demand from courts and the varying circumstances and characteristics of offenders in each area.

3. To ensure that SAO schemes have sufficient appropriate staff, suitable accommodation, and other resources to meet the demands made on them by the courts.

4. To ensure that SAO schemes are managed and developed in a manner which is consistent with local and national guidelines and results in a service which is credible and fair in the eyes of the courts, the community and offenders alike.

4.3 The following discussion attempts to assess the extent to which each of these objectives has been met and is based on court and SAO records, HHD prison statistics and interviews with sentencers, clerks of the court, SAO staff, agencies providing activities and offenders on a SAO.

A. Objectives of the SAO

a) The SAO as an alternative to custody.

4.4 One of the main issues of the pilot has been the extent to which SAOs are being used as an alternative to custody. It must be emphasised that a reliable assessment about the impact of the SAO on sentencing practices or receptions into prison cannot be made until SAO schemes have been running for a longer period of time when numbers will be substantially greater. However, a preliminary assessment can be made on the basis of: a) data obtained during interviews; b) data from court lists; and c) prison statistics.

4.5 Earlier in the report it was stated that many sentencers reported that they were using the

SAO as an alternative to custody; that SAO staff considered that over half of the cases given a SAO might have received a custodial sentence; and that over one third of offenders on a SAO interviewed thought that they would have received a custodial sentence. The statistics presented in Table VI indicated that SAOs may have contributed to the reduction in the proportion of those given a custodial sentence in Ayr since the establishment of the SAO scheme.

4.6   Another route into custody is when the defaulter is given more time to pay with the alternative of a custodial sentence on further default. The proportion given more time plus the alternative in each court did not show a reduction compared to previous years (Table VI). However, there is some evidence to suggest that a greater proportion of those received into custody did so as a result of default when the alternative had been imposed rather than as a result of a direct custodial sentence (Table XVI).

4.7   Table XVI provides: the numbers of receptions into custody for fine default and the number of these which were a first sentence (ie not consecutive to an existing sentence)[1]; and number of cases given a custodial sentence or an alternative between 1989 and 1991 and during the pilot[2].

Table XVI.   Fine Defaulters: Receptions into Custody, Custodial Sentences and the Alternative by Year and Court.

	Ayr Sheriff	Dundee Sheriff	Dundee District	Highland Sheriff
1989				
No. Receptions	232	281	238	45
First Sentence	(not available in 1989)			
Custodial Sentence	-	109	3	3
Alternative imposed	-	424	252	98
1990				
No. Receptions	130	131	131	109
First Sentence	89	109	105	82
Custodial Sentence	76	100	18	35
Alternative imposed	44	127	100	52
1991				
No. Receptions	169	146	186	88
First Sentence	120	123	135	67
Custodial Sentence	121	50	3	29
Alternative imposed	216	241	206	116
1992				
No. Receptions	171	184	180	151
First Sentence	138	150	124	112

---

[1] Source: The Scottish Office Home & Health Dept. unpublished prison statistics

[2] Source: The research findings (court lists)

	Ayr Sh.	Dundee Sh.	Dundee Dis.	Highland Sh.
Pilot (to end December)				
No. Receptions	30	60	56	55
First Sentence	24	49	32	40
Custodial Sentence	18	30	10	8
Alternative imposed	85	139	72	60

4.8   Table XVI clearly demonstrates the reduction in the number of receptions for fine default between 1989 and 1990 in each court (except Highland) followed by an increase in 1991 (except Highland which showed a decrease).   In 1992 the number of receptions from Dundee Sheriff Court and Highland increased.   It is perhaps surprising to see that the number received into custody in 1990 were almost identical for Ayr, Dundee Sheriff and Dundee District Courts.   It is not known why Dundee District Court should have the highest number of receptions in 1991, despite having a similar number of fine defaulters attending court as Ayr Sheriff Court and about 100 less attenders than Dundee Sheriff Court in that year (see Table VI).

4.9   It is evident that almost all prison receptions from Dundee District Court are of those given more time to pay with an alternative of a custodial sentence on default (especially in 1989 and 1991).   Data were extracted from court records on those given a custodial sentence to identify which cases had been received into custody and which had paid their outstanding fine prior to admission to custody. (These data were available for only half of those given a custodial sentence in Dundee Sheriff Court and thus an assessment cannot be made for this court).   It is estimated that the proportion of those given a custodial sentence who are actually received into custody are: 67 per cent for Ayr; 70 per cent for Dundee District Court; and 38 per cent for Highland.   The proportion of those given more time to pay with an alternative custodial sentence on default who are likely to serve the alternative are: 21 per cent for Ayr; 68 per cent for Dundee District Court; and 87 per cent for Highland. Overall, the estimated proportion of all those received into custody who had defaulted having being given more time to pay plus an alternative, are: 60 per cent in Ayr; 87 per cent in Dundee District Court; and 95 per cent in Highland.

4.10   Thus it would appear that, if the SAO is to be implemented as an alternative to a custodial sentence (as is stressed in the SWSG guidelines) and if numbers are to be increased, sentencers should consider very carefully whether those to whom they are likely to give more time to pay plus an alternative on default would be suitable for Supervised Attendance, as the majority of this group (in some courts) end up in prison. Some of those sentencers who were interviewed reported that they did not know what happened to those given more time plus the alternative or how many of those given a custodial sentence paid prior to being admitted to custody.   One sentencer suggested that there should be some sort of screening by a judicial figure of defaulters as they arrive at custody to ensure that those for whom custody was never intended do not 'slip through the net'.   Feedback from interviews with sentencers implied that in some cases the custodial sentence and the alternative were viewed as threats by sentencers to ensure that defaulters paid but in practice it would appear that many did not pay and were admitted to custody.

b)   <u>To provide defaulters with an opportunity to receive a community based penalty</u>

4.11   It could be argued that offenders who have appeared before sentencers who were not aware of the SAO or who were not in favour of this court disposal, were given a limited opportunity to receive this community based penalty.   SAO staff and managers identified the problem of informing and reminding all sentencers of the availability of the SAO. Providing information about the SAO to sentencers, however, does not necessarily ensure their use of this court disposal as some SAO staff suggested that a few sentencers did not have a favourable attitude towards the Order and were unlikely to use it. Only those sentencers who had experience of imposing a SAO were invited to provide their views, thus the research does not have direct access to the views of those who had not used or did not intend to use this disposal. Perhaps resources should be targeted on discussing the SAO with those who have not used this disposal or who are known to be reluctant to use it. Sentencers may be more willing to use the SAO once the initial pilot period has ended when most teething problems will have been resolved and when they can judge whether the SAO is operating satisfactorily.

4.12   It is also appropriate to discuss the extent to which defaulters were provided with the opportunity to decline this disposal (it is a legal requirement that the offender has to accept the conditions of the order). A few defaulters refused to undertake a SAO when offered by the sentencer. Figures are not accurate but SAO staff estimated that approximately eight offenders refused in Dundee, as the offenders preferred to do the time and "get it over and done with" rather than serving 40 hours which could "seem like an eternity". A few defaulters had refused a SAO in Ayr up until the end of January and it was not known how many had refused in Highland. Two of those offenders on a SAO who were interviewed reported that they were not given the opportunity to decline a SAO - one said that he had the money with him at court to pay the fine and another said that he had not been given the opportunity to explain his circumstances.

c)   Discipline, Supervision and Breach

4.13   The third objective of the SAO is to ensure that SAOs are characterised by the imposition of discipline on the offender and firm and reliable supervision including the expeditious institution of breach proceedings. The first part of this objective can be measured by providing statistics on the number of absences (Table XV), lateness and unsatisfactory behaviour. It is recognised, however, that some discretion may have been exercised by supervisors and SAO staff in classifying absences, lateness and behaviour as unacceptable (such discretion is permitted within the guidelines). Paragraphs 1.7 and 1.8 outline the formal policy relating to procedures and criteria to be used in discipline and breach. The criteria generally applied for acceptable absences or lateness in each scheme was if the offender had provided prior notification or if it was a genuine emergency. Classification of unacceptable behaviour is less clear-cut than unacceptable absences but usually applies to those who have disregarded a warning about no smoking or who have displayed disruptive behaviour.

(i)   Unacceptable absences

4.14   SAO staff reported a strict interpretation of the guidelines in terms of visiting those who failed to attend during the same day as the absence or within 24 hours, if possible. A formal warning would be issued although SAO staff did, however, choose to use their discretion in delaying breach in a few cases when they thought that the threat of breach might motivate the offender to complete his/her Order. In one such case, the offender continued not to attend and was breached, resulting in a 40-hour order.

4.15   APEX reported that about 80 per cent of offenders received one or two warnings at the beginning of the Order, often because of a failure to attend the first interview, but that once they started to attend activities they settled down and were more reliable. A few social work managers stressed the need to get the offender started on the Order quickly as the experience with Community Service Orders showed that once offenders begin to drift, it often results in breach. The interval between the date of imposition of the order and the date when activities commenced was less than one week in about half of all cases from Ayr, Dundee Sheriff and the District Courts, more than three-quarters of those from Perth, none of those from Highland and 47 per cent over all schemes. About one third of those from Ayr, Dundee District and Highland, and the remaining cases from Perth, commenced within two weeks. Of those offenders where a warrant for breach was issued, three had commenced their Order seven days after the date of imposition of the SAO, one at ten days, one at twelve days and one at 30 days. Although the number of breach warrants is too low on which to base any conclusion about a link between delays prior to commencement of the Order and breach, it is worth noting that delays can be caused by factors outwith the direct control of the SAO staff or the offender, such as the severe flooding in Dundee and snow in Inverness, closure of the SAO offices during the Christmas holidays and the offender being admitted to custody on another charge and illness.

(ii)   Unacceptable behaviour

4.16   In Ayr, the scheme which had used the most agencies during the research period, SAO staff deal with disciplinary problems but also provide agencies with advice on how to handle such problems, if the agency requests this assistance. SAO staff in Ayr also attended a few agency sessions to be available to provide support if required although SAO staff said that there was a certain amount of peer group pressure to conform when someone was disruptive during a session.

4.17   The number of instances of recorded unpunctuality was exceedingly small in all schemes and it is not known whether this reflects a true level, whether supervisors did not regularly record such instances or whether these were not reported to the researcher. SAO staff in one scheme reported that they changed reporting procedures to suit the circumstances of one agency so that SAO staff contacted the agency ten minutes after the start of a session to check on absences and lateness, rather than waiting for the agency to contact them which, on a few occasions, was not until the following day. There were seven recorded instances of being late in Ayr (4 persons); four in Dundee Sheriff Court (3 persons); none recorded from Dundee District Court; nine instances in Highland (four people); and none from Perth. None of these were considered to be acceptable reasons for being late. The number of instances of unsatisfactory behaviour in Ayr was seven (3 related to alcohol, 2 to the offenders' lack of co-operation with the activity supervisor and 2 to lacking co-operation with others in the group); none in Dundee Sheriff Court; one in Dundee District Court (drugs); 2 in Highland (not following instructions); and none in Perth.

(iii)   Views of Sentencers, SAO Staff, Agency Staff and Offenders.

4.18   Sentencers seemed to be satisfied about the level of supervision and the institution of breach proceedings, although most said it was too early to make a proper assessment. Sentencers indicated that they would treat each breach case on its own merit and that a custodial sentence would not necessarily be imposed on breach. The legislation allows sentencers to either impose a custodial sentence on breach or vary the number of hours specified in the Order. One sentencer stressed the importance of invoking breach proceedings rapidly.

4.19   Most sentencers and SAO staff thought that the community was not yet aware of SAOs and were unlikely to have any views on supervision and breach. (However, there had been some local and national publicity about each scheme and some letters from the public were published in the newspapers, one complaining about a SAO offender getting off without paying for his fine but managing to go to the pub and another which supported the SAO as a better and cheaper alternative to custody). All but three offenders in Ayr and Dundee thought that discipline was good most of the time in the sessions which they attended.

4.20   Most agencies reported that they had not experienced any problems about discipline or invoking breach proceedings. Two agencies in two schemes considered that SAO staff should be more strict in relation to the implementation of breach proceedings. One agency said that breach does not automatically follow three unacceptable absences and that there appeared to be "a degree of leniency before action is taken". In another scheme, an agency considered that "sometimes offenders are given more latitude than need be but this is done with the best of intentions to get them through the Order".

4.21   The SAO staff in one scheme suggested that perhaps those on a long Order (60 hours) could be allowed more formal warnings prior to breach as non-attendances tended to occur in the early stages or that offenders could "work off" a warning by, for example, attending for a month without any problems.

4.22   It is evident that the SAO has been characterised by the imposition of discipline on the offender through the requirement to attend his/her placement on a regular basis, to behave satisfactorily and to undertake and participate in the defined activity in a proper fashion. Applications have been made to court for breach after three formal warnings but SAO staff have in some cases delayed breach to give the offender another chance to complete the Order.

d)   Constructive Activities

4.23   SAO staff in each of the models felt that SAO activities were constructive, some because they were of benefit to the individual or the community or because it is a more constructive disposal than custody. It was suggested that it was a more constructive use of time than hanging around street corners and that in the long-term what they learn may be of some use to them. It is interesting to note that SAO staff tended to identify leisure and recreation activities or unpaid work as examples of constructive activities, rather than the educational aspects which were viewed more as of benefit to the individual, although one SAO officer did feel that these would be seen to be constructive in the long term. The unpaid work in the Highland scheme was thought to appeal to the community more than the educational model and be seen as constructive by them. Sentencers and clerks thought the SAO was constructive because the offender avoided custody, was a 'constructive' use of time and if the community benefited. Some sentencers felt that it was too early to make any assessments. One justice thought that the core module aspect of the SAO was especially constructive as it addressed many of the offender's problems and any acquisition of information and skills was bound to be for the good. Another justice also thought the core module to be good training for offenders.

4.24   Two thirds of the offenders who were interviewed thought that the SAO should be a combination of all three aspects. Some of the reasons provided included: "it makes the SAO more interesting and gives more choice"; "it prevents it from being very boring"; "it would make it more punishing"; and "you could learn more". All the agencies who were interviewed thought that the activities were constructive, the main reasons being because: the activities are practical; the topic was relevant to the offender's situation (especially money management); the offenders are learning something useful and are learning a new skill.

4.25   Specific examples (provided by SAO staff) of how offenders have benefited from their SAO included: applying for a desktop publishing course which the offender had heard about from a Community Education module; learning that he was entitled to additional benefits after a Welfare Rights module; progressing on to APEX's mainstream training project; attending a job club; joining a sports centre and offenders offering their services on a voluntary basis.

4.26   It is evident that the majority of those involved in the schemes consider the activities (whether educational, constructive use of time or unpaid work) as constructive.

B.   Operational Objectives

a)   Integration into Social Work Services

4.27   In each scheme, the SAOs are organised and managed as an integral part of social work services provided by local authorities in relation to the criminal justice system. In Highland, the scheme is organised by those responsible for Community Service Orders and is fully integrated with services for Community Service and other offenders.   In Ayr, the SAO staff report to the District Co-ordinator (Offender Services) and in Dundee the SAO staff report to the Principal Officer (Offender Services) and it is planned that the social work responsibilities within the scheme will be undertaken by social work area teams.

b)   Range of Activities

4.28   The second operational objective was to 'ensure that a sufficient range of activity opportunities are provided to meet the expected demand from courts and the varying circumstances and characteristics of offenders in each area'.   The relatively low number of Orders has meant that there has not been a problem in finding sufficient activities but there were problems in arranging sessions for a small number of offenders. SAO staff in each scheme are confident that they can meet an increase in demand as they already have other activities and agencies prepared to provide activities and would be able to find additional activities if necessary.

4.29   Each scheme has proved to be flexible in that each has arranged for individual placements for at least one offender with special needs or circumstances which do not readily suit the available activities, for example those with employment or other commitments. None of the agencies thought that the activities they offer would exclude any types of offender except those whose previous offences might warrant it, for example, someone with a history of violence would not participate in the joinery workshop but could be accommodated in some of the other activities.

c)   Staffing and Other Resources

4.30   Each scheme would appear to have sufficient appropriate staff, suitable accommodation and other resources to meet the present demands of the courts, but the schemes had just expanded into district courts at the time of interviews and the flow of Orders had not increased dramatically by that stage.   There was some doubt as to whether the present staffing levels in each scheme would support holiday and sickness absences.   Until schemes have developed further, it is difficult to predict whether they will have sufficient resources to met an increase in demand.

d)   Credibility and Fairness

4.31   The final operational objective is 'to ensure that SAO schemes are managed and developed in a manner which is consistent with local and national guidelines and results in a service which is credible and fair in the eyes of the courts, the community and offenders alike'. The extent to which each scheme has been developed in a manner consistent with the national guidelines will be discussed in the next chapter.   One aspect which could be considered unfair (but which was not identified as such by SAO staff or offenders during interviews) was the practice of crediting the time of the post-sentence interviews in Ayr and Tayside to the SAO but not in Highland. It is understood that this practice has now terminated in Ayr and that the post-sentence interviews (SAO and APEX) in Tayside have been reduced from 2.5 hours to one hour but that this hour is still credited to the Order.

(i)   Sentencers' Views

4.32   In as much as some sentencers are using this court disposal, consider activities to be constructive, have no criticisms of the level of discipline and supervision as yet and did not mention any adverse comments about the different models of SAO scheme, it could perhaps be concluded that these sentencers view the SAO as credible and fair. As views were not obtained from those who had not imposed a SAO, it is possible that some of these sentencers did not view the SAO as a credible disposal.

(ii)   Offenders' Views

4.33   Only two offenders thought that the number of hours imposed were not fair in relation to other offenders on a SAO who had more to pay but less hours to serve. (Two-thirds thought that the level of original fine imposed was not fair in relation to what they could afford and 41% thought that the outcomes of the FECs were not fair). We have seen that a rough tariff system seemed to be operating in the Highland and Tayside schemes, with sentencers exercising their right to use their discretion.

4.34   None of the offenders mentioned any problems arising from the operation of different models of Supervised Attendance but some of the SAO staff and managers agreed that the provision of different types of activities between schemes was unfair to offenders (although offenders did not perceive it as such), was confusing and in the future may cause problems on transfers between schemes, as the offender has agreed to the specific type of Order of that scheme.

4.35   It would appear that the majority of offenders thought that the SAO was a credible court disposal. All but two offenders said that they would rather have carried out a SAO than have gone to prison. Over half of the offenders who participated in educational activities said that they were interested in all of the topics, the remainder finding one or more topics uninteresting or boring, although almost all offenders thought that the topics had been well presented and that they had learnt something.

4.36   Only one of the 21 offenders who participated in activities relating to 'constructive use of time' did not find these activities interesting and only four said that they did not learn anything, mainly because they already knew how to do these activities. Two of the ten offenders interviewed who had undertaken unpaid work were not interested in the work; about half thought that they had learnt something; two-thirds said they had benefited from the experience and all of these offenders said that others had benefited from the work.

4.37   Only four of the 58 offenders who were interviewed said that they would not want to do a SAO again and eight said that with a future fine they might decide to default in the hope of getting a SAO, the remainder saying that they would attempt to pay the fine. The reasons given for wanting to do it again included: "it's better than jail"; "you learn something"; "it's easier than finding the money for the fine"; and "it's a challenge and a chance to help others".

4.38   When asked about the worst things about their SAO, two offenders complained of being treated like a child or being patronised at one session, which was later changed to avoid this criticism.   Other factors mentioned included: "some talks were boring"; "the whole thing was a waste of time - I could have been doing better things" (one offender only); "being on time"; "having to take orders"; "no smoking".   The things which the offenders liked best about their SAO included: "getting the fine off my back"; "talking to people"; "SAO staff helped you if you had problems"; "learning something"; "helping other people"; "meeting new people"; "keeps you out of prison"; and "I liked it all".

4.39   The feedback from interviews with offenders demonstrates the relatively high level of support which they had for the SAO and it would thus appear that most offenders thought that it was a credible and fair disposal.

Conclusion

4.40   This chapter has provided an assessment of the extent to which the objectives of the SAO, as stated in the SWSG guidelines, have been met.

   a)   Use of the SAO as an Alternative to Custody

   1. Estimates of the numbers of SAOs being imposed as an alternative to custody vary between one third (offenders' views) to over three quarters (SAO staff views). Sentencers' views ranged from none to all.

   2. An analysis of court records showed that sentencers in Ayr seem to be using the SAO as an alternative to custody.

   3. Between 60 and 95 per cent of receptions to custody for fine default were not given a direct custodial sentence but were given the alternative on default of more time to pay.

   b)   To Provide Offenders with an Opportunity to Receive a Community-based Penalty

   4. It could be said that not all defaulters are being given an opportunity to receive this community-based penalty, as some sentencers may not have been aware of or have remembered about this new court disposal.

   c)   Characteristics of the SAO

   5. The imposition of discipline on the offender through the requirement to attend the placement on a regular basis (the number of unacceptable absences as a rate per 100 completed hours was very low (3 to 8) except in Perth where the rate was 27) and to behave satisfactorily (there were very few recorded instances of lateness or unsatisfactory behaviour).

   6. Firm and reliable supervision - most sentencers, agencies and offenders considered that the level of discipline had been high. The number of applications for breach was low (six) and in only three cases did SAO staff delay breach to enable the offender to receive another chance to complete the Order.

   7. Most sentencers and all the SAO staff considered the activities to be constructive because the offender avoided custody; the activities were a constructive use of time; and when the community or individual benefited. Agencies thought that activities were constructive because the topics were relevant to the individual's situation (especially money management) and that the offenders were learning something useful.

d)   <u>Operational Objectives</u>

8. The SAOs were seen to be organised and managed as an integral part of social work services. There was also a sufficient range of activities to meet the demand from courts and the varying circumstances and characteristics of offenders in each area. Sufficient staff and resources were available to meet the demands at that time but it was not known whether these would meet any future increase in demand.

9. Most of the sentencers who had used the SAO viewed it as credible and fair, as did most offenders (the educational activities and constructive use of time activities were found to be interesting and well presented and they felt that they learnt something, the unpaid work was seen by them as constructive as they learnt and benefited from the work as did the community).

10. The main criticism in relation to the fairness of SAOs, came from some SAO staff who thought that having three models was not fair to offenders, especially those who might get transferred to another scheme, and that the community service-type model confused the identity of the SAO. The practice of crediting the post-sentence interview to SAO hours in Tayside but not in the other schemes, may also be viewed as unfair.

11. The majority of offenders would agree to a SAO in the future and thought that it was a good court disposal and much better than going to prison. The feedback from offenders indicated that they viewed the SAO as credible and fair.

5. EVALUATION OF THE EFFECTIVENESS OF THE GUIDELINES

5.1   One of the aims of the research was to assist in the revision of the guidelines into National Standards, leading to the research objective of evaluating the operational effectiveness and value of the guidelines.   This chapter outlines the main areas where practice or views conflict with the recommendations set out in the guidelines.

5.2   Most sentencers who were interviewed (or had returned the self-completion questionnaire) had read the SWSG guidelines and considered them to be useful, except two, who felt that they would be of use to social workers but not themselves (it is acknowledged that the guidelines are not prepared for the judiciary).   One sentencer reported that he relied on the social workers to tell him if he was doing anything wrong.   One sheriff clerk found the guidelines useful when devising the leaflet to be given to defaulters.   None of the sentencers or clerks had any comments about the need for changes to the guidelines.

Legislation and Method of Introduction

a)   Legislation

5.3   There has been some criticism of the legislation.   The guidelines state that "a court may make a Supervised Attendance Order only where an offender defaults in payment of any part or instalment of a fine".   One sheriff clerk advised sheriffs in early 1993 not to impose a SAO if the defaulter also had a Compensation Order because the legislation referred to fines only.   As many fine defaulters who might be considered suitable for a SAO in that court also have a Compensation Order, there were very few new orders made in that court in the months following the research fieldwork.   During the period until the end of January 1993, 13 offenders on a SAO overall (12% of all offenders on a SAO) were serving a Compensation Order.   One social work manager considered that it should be possible to impose a SAO on the fine and retain the Compensation Order so that the victim does not lose out.   He suggested that a financial assessment (possibly a questionnaire administered by SAO staff) could identify whether the offender would be able to pay the compensation, and if not, that a SAO could be imposed for both the fine and Compensation Order in such cases.

5.4   Some sentencers and sheriff clerks stated that the legislation was not clear enough in some respects, for example, the legislation did not specify whether the SAO discharged the fine totally or whether an offender could pay off his fine if breached for the SAO and if so, whether SAO hours completed would be credited.   Others wondered whether completed SAO hours would be credited when a decision was made regarding length of custodial sentence on breach.

5.5   There was considerable support amongst sentencers and SAO staff for extending the SAO to the position of a primary disposal.   It was suggested that some sentencers may give someone a fine, knowing that he would default, so that the sentencer could consider a SAO. More than three-quarters of offenders said that the level of fine imposed was greater than they could afford (although it was not clear whether this was in relation to instalments or the total fine), two thirds had other debts and about half said that their debts had not been taken into consideration at the FEC.   Many sentencers and SAO staff thought that a person should not be fined if they have no visible means of support and that a SAO as a primary disposal would be preferable.   One justice and SAO officer thought that the SAO as a primary disposal would require a Social Enquiry Report assessment which would make it a more expensive disposal.   A few offenders, when asked for any other comments, suggested that the SAO should be a primary disposal. One SAO officer suggested that SAO as a primary disposal would save the costs and emotional stress to the offender by avoiding the necessity of attending a FEC and returning again on default. Other SAO staff thought that the SAO would be an appropriate first disposal for 16-18 year olds who do not have the money to pay a fine.

b)   Tariff

5.6   The guidelines suggest that "The court may wish to take into consideration the prison term it could have imposed . . . . . in determining the number of hours of Supervised Attendance to impose". As discussed earlier in the report, some sentencers would welcome a broad tariff scale and were disappointed that such a scale was not contained in the legislation or the guidelines, whereas other sentencers did not propose to apply a tariff. The research data did indicate that a broad tariff scale was in operation but not consistently and that two offenders complained of inconsistent lengths of Order. If the SAO is to be seen as a fair and consistent disposal, it would be desirable to include a tariff scale in the guidelines to satisfy those sentencers who sought some guidance on number of hours in relation to amount of fine outstanding.

c)   Introduction of Supervised Attendance Orders

5.7   On the basis of the experience of the pilot schemes, vigorous efforts are required to remind sentencers, clerks and solicitors of the availability of the SAO and to inform visiting sentencers of this disposal. This should be stressed in the guidelines. The presence of SAO staff in the court during the initial stages may also assist although it may not appear to be an efficient use of time. Sentencers reported that they welcomed the social work presence in the court and SAO staff said that visiting sheriffs were still not fully conversant with the scheme and appreciated the social work presence.

d)   Demand

5.8   The number of Orders imposed in each scheme was far short of the number which social work managers had estimated. The estimated level of demand would appear to have been partly based on an economically viable level rather than on expected numbers.   It is important for schemes to take into account the relatively low number of Orders which can be expected in the first few months (plans for group activities may be jeopardised by low numbers in the initial stages) and this should be noted in the guidelines.

e)   Liaison with Courts

5.9   The guidelines stress the importance of local authorities discussing with sentencers: the guidelines, the range of available activities, the kinds of offender for whom provision can be made and likely level of demand. The research showed that SAO staff considered that the type of offender considered suitable for a SAO was the sentencer's responsibility and that sentencers considered the remainder to be the SAO staff's responsibility and wished only to be informed rather than to enter into discussions about these aspects. The wording in the guidelines should perhaps be altered to reflect this.

The National Guidelines

5.10   Chapter 2 of the guidelines states that the aim of the guidelines is to "establish bench marks against which consistency and good management practice can be tested . . " and to encourage managerial flexibility and initiative and professional judgement. SWSG encouraged the development of three quite different models for the pilot whereby defaulters in Highland undertake community service type work whilst defaulters in the other schemes participate in educational activities, those that can be described as constructive use of time, and in Tayside, some unpaid work.

5.11   Those involved in the Tayside scheme considered that their model was ideal, a mixture of all three elements, which they thought was more flexible than the community service model, as they could operate on a surgery basis, taking the SAO activities to the offenders in Perth and Arbroath, for example. However, it was pointed out that this could delay the start of the Order until the APEX staff were due to visit and could extend the length of time to complete an Order. The number of offenders would need to be relatively high to make this cost-efficient and if the delays were to cause problems, such as more absences or breaches, additional staff may be required for these areas. The presentation of the core module on a one-to-one basis would appear to be costly.

5.12   All the sentencers interviewed in Tayside proposed the combination of the three elements. One justice thought that the more offenders are taught, the more likely they are to avoid re-offending and another justice thought that the counselling and guidance were important but that skills should be encouraged and that public acceptance would be greater if it is felt that offenders are 'paying their debt' by completing unpaid work for the benefit of the community. A third justice considered the educational aspect useful for those who cannot budget but for others, non-payment had nothing to do with inability to manage a budget and that their SAO should be more a 'fine on their time' than educational. One sheriff in Tayside considered that the provision of all three elements allowed the SAO to be imposed on a wide variety of offenders.

5.13   The SAO staff and managers in the Ayr scheme considered that their model was ideal: a combination of educational activities and constructive use of time. It was suggested that, if this model can work in south Ayrshire which has urban centres and a large rural area, then it can work in similar areas in Scotland. One of the advantages of this model is the involvement of the community through the extensive use of local agencies to provide most of the activities. The wide range of activities allows for a certain choice for individuals and provides variety for those on long Orders. SAO staff claimed that the model was very flexible as modules could be dropped or introduced to suit the numbers and needs of those serving their orders. The courts thought that the scheme should perhaps be a combination of all three elements which would allow the Order to be tailor-made to suit the individual as some might need education, some training and others community work.

5.14   Highland claimed that their scheme was easier to set up and would be cheaper to run. They considered that they could not run a group in sparsely-populated areas and to bring offenders to a centre would be very costly in terms of time and fares. SAO staff were confident that sentencers would not impose SAOs if activities were educational. One sheriff thought that it should be principally unpaid work but that some offenders might benefit from education and constructive use of time. A sheriff clerk thought that it should only be unpaid work, as this would be of benefit to the community and would allow the individual to feel they had contributed something worthwhile.

5.15   It is evident that the existence of the three models has resulted in a very different experience for those given a SAO in each area. Policy makers should consider whether such differences reflect the geographical and cultural characteristics of the area (bearing in mind that Highland and Ayr both face the problem of scattered communities and poor public transport yet have developed very different schemes) or whether these differences undermine the identity of the SAO and a more limited range of models should be encouraged in the future.

Activities For Offenders

5.16 The guidelines state that offenders should not undertake more than 20 hours unpaid work or that not more than 50 per cent of their order should be unpaid work unless it is not possible to arrange any other form of supervised activity due to the characteristics of the offender, the nature of the offence or the geographical nature of the area where the offender lives. The Highland scheme, however, consists mainly of unpaid work although none of the offenders on a SAO lived far from a SAO centre and could have participated in educational group activities if these had been provided. If it is decided that the Community Service-type model should continue to operate, the guidelines should be changed to allow for this level of unpaid work. However, interviews with offenders on a SAO from Highland identified that many would prefer a more varied range of activities.

5.17 The guidelines state that the nature of the activity must be kept distinct from that undertaken by Community Service offenders although it would appear that the unpaid work undertaken in Highland and some of that undertaken in Tayside is similar to that undertaken by Community Service offenders.

5.18 Both Tayside and the Ayr schemes followed the guidelines' suggestion that each Order commence with a mandatory core induction period. We have seen how the low number of Orders and the fact that the core module was split between two (and now three) centres, resulted in the Ayr scheme abandoning the mandatory core module at the beginning of the order, although offenders did participate in some of these sessions throughout their Order. Tayside's decision to provide sessions on a one-to-one basis allowed them to continue with the mandatory core module at the beginning of the Order. However, individual sessions may not be as beneficial as group sessions which allow for more discussion and motivation. It has been suggested that core module sessions as a block at the beginning of the Order could be very boring for offenders and that they might find them more interesting if these were dispersed throughout the Order, as in the Ayr scheme. As the core module covers 10 hours, those on a short Order in Tayside do not experience any other type of activity, whereas if these sessions were dispersed throughout the Order, and those on a short Order had to do a minimum of two core modules, the Order might become more interesting to offenders and may lead to less absences.

5.19 The guidelines suggest that consideration regarding the venue of activities should include whether offenders could be exposed to other activities going on there (eg at a community centre or further education college). During the research period there was only one instance of an activity being part of a community activity (at a sports centre), which proved most successful (the offender's self-esteem increased and he was accepted as part of the group although they did not know he was on a SAO). Schemes should perhaps consider using existing community activities which would enhance the value of the SAO as a community-based penalty.

Working Arrangements

a)   Pre-sentence Procedures

5.20 The guidelines state that the clerk of court should enclose an explanatory leaflet about SAOs with the citation to a FEC. There were various views about whether this is necessary as offenders do not receive a leaflet about the Community Service Order, although it was also argued that the offender receives pre-sentence assessment which includes an explanation of Community Service. It was decided that the leaflet would not be sent out with the citation at Dundee Sheriff Court but would be sent out by the other courts. The guidance in the guidelines should perhaps be reconsidered.

b)   Other Post-sentence Procedures

5.21   The SAO staff in each scheme stressed the importance of getting the offender started on his Order as soon as possible after the Order was imposed as the experience with community service was that this reduced the chances of breach. They considered that the 14-day rule (stated in the guidelines) between receipt of the Order and the post-sentence interview with the offender was probably too lenient and should be reduced. A shorter interval between the order and the post-sentence interview could be stated in the guidelines but allowing an extension in exceptional circumstances such as the offender being in custody or when a previous SAO has not been completed.

5.22   One area of inconsistency between the schemes was that Ayr and Tayside credited the duration of the post-sentence interview to the Order whilst the Highland interview was not credited.   This practice has now been terminated in Ayr but continues in Tayside.   The guidelines should ensure that offenders are treated equally and that this time is either credited in each scheme or in none.

5.23   The guidelines state the minimum time periods of attendance for each length of Order and recommends that the maximum attendance should be 10 hours or two sessions per week. SAO and agency staff views on the ideal length of sessions depended on the type of activity undertaken. It was generally thought that 2.5 hours was the maximum length for an educational activity, although some agencies thought that this was too long for some young offenders whose concentration span was short. At the other extreme, Highland preferred a 5 or 7-hour session in one day to reduce travel time and that this was possible with unpaid work. SAO staff did, however, use their discretion and in certain circumstances allowed offenders to undertake more than 10 hours in one week or do more than two sessions.

Requirements of the Order and Compliance

5.24   It is recommended that any absence should be followed up within 4 working days of notification but SAO staff set themselves the target of a maximum of two days and attempted to visit the offender within 24 hours. Perhaps the guidelines should take account of this.

5.25   It would appear that Highland might sometimes be issuing a first formal warning on the second unacceptable absence and that there seems to be a certain amount of discretion being applied amongst schemes regarding instituting breach proceedings after the third unacceptable absence or third formal warning. The guidelines do not specifically state that SAO staff can exercise their discretion in relation to absences (although it does exist in relation to unsatisfactory behaviour) and perhaps this should be clarified.

Monitoring and Evaluation

5.26   In addition to the information systems required by SWSG, each scheme has introduced an evaluation procedure in which offenders comment on each session.   This feedback has proved particularly valuable to the Tayside and Ayr schemes in relation to the educational activities and the presentation and content of many of the topics have been amended in light of the offenders' views. The Highland scheme has mainly followed its well-tested procedures for its community service programme, whereas the Ayr and Tayside schemes were testing innovative procedures and activities. They have been shown to have adopted a very flexible approach, learning from mistakes and developing the scheme to suit the circumstances of and feedback from offenders who were given a SAO.

6. CONCLUSION

6.1 The aims of the research were to monitor and evaluate the establishment and operation of the pilot schemes and national guidelines, to assist the revision of the guidelines into National Standards and to inform the design of further schemes.

6.2 It must be emphasised that this study examined the setting up and initial stages of the pilot schemes and thus the results (based on a relatively low number of SAOs and covering only a few months of operation), regarding the impact of the Supervised Attendance Order on sentencing practices, for example, relate only to the early stages of the schemes and cannot be assumed to reflect the operation and 'success' of the SAO in the following years.

6.3 The main issues raised by the research include:

a) <u>The different models adopted by each scheme</u>
Does the SAO lose its identity when one scheme adopts a mini-Community Service model, another works in partnership with local organisations to provide activities and the third employs a voluntary organisation (APEX) to manage the activities? Should different models be allowed to develop or should schemes be encouraged to adopt a more consistent approach?

b) <u>Estimates of demand in the initial stages</u>
New schemes should recognise that the use of a new court disposal is likely to be low in the first few months until sentencers acquaint themselves with procedures and gain confidence about levels of supervision and discipline and the viability of the disposal. To encourage greater use of Supervised Attendance, SAO staff should be aware of the need to 'market' the SAO to sentencers and solicitors, by explaining the operation of the Order and by reminding (especially visiting) sentencers of its availability in that court.

c) <u>The use of the SAO as an alternative to a custodial sentence</u>
Whilst there was statistical evidence to support the hypothesis that the introduction of the SAO influenced the proportion of defaulters given a custodial sentence in Ayr Sheriff Court, further research should be undertaken in other courts once a greater number of Orders have been imposed, to assess the extent to which the SAO is being used as an alternative to a custodial sentence or as a useful additional court disposal.

d) <u>The 'success' of the SAO in the initial pilot period</u>
An assessment of 'success' of the SAO during its early stages was undertaken by evaluating the SAO in relation to its objectives. Despite the short period of research and the low numbers of Orders imposed, an initial assessment showed that the introduction of Supervised Attendance was successful. Although an evaluation of the success of the SAO as a well-established court disposal would require further research after at least one year of operation in each court, the main criteria for success of the SAO in the early stages include the following:

- Supervised Attendance Orders were being imposed.
- Orders were successfully completed.
- Discipline was imposed and applications for breach were made for those offenders who did not comply with the conditions of the Order.
- Many sentencers, offenders and representatives of local agencies providing activities regarded the SAO as a fair and constructive court disposal.

6.4   It is suggested that further research might address some of the following questions:

- Is the SAO being used as an alternative to a custodial sentence or as an alternative to being given more time to pay?

- Has any change occurred in the proportion of receptions of fine defaulters to custody as a result of an immediate custodial sentence as opposed to being given the alternative of custody on default of more time to pay?

- Since the introduction of the SAO has the rate of receptions of fine defaulters to custody decreased?

- What are the main reasons for sentencers not using the SAO?

- In what ways do offenders on a SAO differ from defaulters given a custodial sentence or more time to pay?

- Have schemes adopted a consistent approach to discipline and instituting breach proceedings?

- Are there any factors which may be more likely to lead to breach, such as delay between the imposition of the Order and starting activities?

- What are the main areas of good practice?

6.5   It is hoped that, despite the limitations of this study regarding a comprehensive evaluation of the SAO as an established court disposal, the report provides a useful adjunct to the development of policy and practice, most especially in relation to the revision of the guidelines into National Standards, and provides a useful reference for social work departments considering establishing a scheme in their area.

CRU RESEARCH - RECENTLY PUBLISHED WORK

The Measurement of Changes in Road Safety : A Consultant's Report by the Ross Silcock Partnership. (1991) *(£5.00)*

Socio-legal Research in the Scottish Courts - Volume 2 : Michael Adler and Ann Millar. (1991) *(£4.00)*

Crime Prevention in Scotland - Findings from the 1988 British Crime Survey : David M Allen and Douglas Payne. (1991) *(£4.00)*

The Public and the Police in Scotland - Findings from the 1988 British Crime Survey : David M Allen and Douglas Payne. (1991) *(£4.00)*

Ethnic Minorities in Scotland : Patten Smith (Social and Community Planning Research). (1991) *(£8.50)*

Adoption and Fostering - The Outcome of Permanent Family Placements in Two Scottish Local Authorities. (1991) *(£5.50)*

Adoption Services in Scotland - A Summary : Recent Research Findings and their Implications: John Triseliotis (Edinburgh University). (1991) *(£4.00)*

Children with Epilepsy and their Families - Needs and Services : A Laybourn and M Hill (Glasgow University). (1991) *(£4.00)*

Community Ownership in Glasgow - An Evaluation : David Clapham, Keith Kintrea and Leslie Whitefield (Centre for Housing Research, Glasgow University), Frances Macmillan and Norman Raitt (Norman Rait Architects, Edinburgh). (1991) *(£12.50)*

Small Claims in the Sheriff Court in Scotland - An Assessment of the Use and Operation of Procedure : Helen Jones, Alison Platts, Jacqueline Tombs (CRU); Cowan Irvine, James McManus (University of Dundee); Kenneth Miller, Alan Paterson (University of Strathclyde). (1991) *(£5.00)*

Physical Evaluation of Community Ownership Schemes : Frances Macmillan and Norman Raitt (Norman Raitt Architects, Edinburgh). (1991) *(£10.00)*

The Impact of Environmental Design Upon the Incidence and Type of Crime - A Literature Review : Jonathan Bannister (Centre for Housing Research, Glasgow University). (1991) *(£5.00)*

Preventing Vehicle Theft - A Policy-Oriented View of the Literature : Ronald V Clarke (State University of New Jersey). (1991) *(£4.00)*

The Location of Alcohol Use by Young People - A Review of the Literature : Neil Hutton (School of Law, Strathclyde University). (1991)

Setting up Community Care Projects - A Practice Guide: Anne Connor. (1991)

Local Authority Housing Stock Transfers : Tom Duncan

(The Planning Exchange, Glasgow). (1991) *(£4.50)*

Competitive Tendering in Scotland - A Survey of Satisfaction with Local Authority Services : A Consultant's Report by The MVA Consultancy. (1991) *(£4.00)*

Public Attitudes to the Environment in Scotland : Diana Wilkinson and Jennifer Waterton. (1991) *(£4.00)*

Text Creation in the Scottish Office - The Experience, Expectations and Perceptions of the Users and Providers of Services: (A report on surveys of four groups of Scottish Office staff carried out by The Special Projects Branch of The Scottish Office Central Research Unit as part of an Efficiency Scrutiny of Text Creation in The Scottish Office): Hugh Gentleman and Susan A Hughes. (1992)

Where the Time Goes - The Allocation of Administration and Casework Between Client Groups in Scottish Departments of Social Work : John Tibbit and Pauline Martin. (1992) *(£4.00)*

Financial Management of Mentally Incapacitated Adults - Characteristics of Curatories : Fiona Rutherdale. (1992) *(£4.00)*

Evaluation of the Care and Repair Initiative in Scotland - Study Report : PIEDA and Norman Rait Architects. (1992) *(£5.00)*

Register of Research (1992-93 Edition) : (1992)

The Hidden Safety Net ? - Mental Health Guardianship: Achievements and Limitations : Carole Moore, Anne Connor, Pauline Martin and John Tibbitt. (1992) *(£5.00)*

Crime in Scotland - Findings from the 1988 British Crime Survey : Douglas Payne. (1992) *(£4.00)*

Crime and the Quality of Life - Public Perceptions and Experiences of Crime in Scotland: Findings from the 1988 British Crime Survey : Richard Kinsey and Simon Anderson. (1992) *(£4.00)*

The Deferred Sentence in Scotland : Linda Nicolson. (1992) *(£5.00)*

Social Work Department Reviews of Children in Care : Andrew Kendrick and Elizabeth Mapstone. (1992) *(£10.00)*

Retail Impact Assessment Methodologies : Consultant's Report by Drivers Jonas, Glasgow. (1992) *(£6.00)*

Section 50 Agreements : Consultant's Report by Jeremy Rowan Robinson and Roger Durman. (1992) *(£6.00)*

Evaluation of Scottish Road Safety Year 1990: Jennifer Waterton. (1992) *(£5.00)*

The Witness in the Scottish Criminal Justice System : Anne Stafford and Stewart Asquith. (1992) *(£4.00)*

Good Practice in Housing Management - A Literature Review : Mary Taylor & Fiona Russell, Dept. of Applied Social Science, Dr Rob Ball , Dept. of Management Science, University of Stirling (in association with The Institute of Housing in Scotland). (1992) *(£4.00)*

Sexual History and Sexual Character Evidence in Scottish Sexual Offence Trials - A Study of Scottish Court Practice under ss. 141A/141B and 346A/346B of the Criminal Procedure (Scotland) Act 1975 as inserted by the Law Reform (Miscellaneous Provisions)(Scotland) Act 1985 s. 36 : Beverley Brown, Michelle Burman and Lynn Jamieson. (1992) *(£4.50)*

Neighbourhood Watch - A Literature Review : Louise Brown. (1992) *(£4.00)*

Strathclyde Police Red Light Initiative - Accident Monitor : MVA Consultancy in association with Jennifer Waterton. (1992) *(£5.00)*

The Rent to Mortgage Scheme in Scotland : Helen Kay and Jeremy Hardin. (1992) *(£4.00)*

Probation In Scotland - Policy and Practice : Roslyn Ford, Jason Ditton and Ann Laybourn. (1992) *(£5.00)*

The Probation Alternative - Case Studies in the Establishment of Alternative to Custody Schemes in Scotland: Anne Creamer, Linda Hartley and Bryan Williams. (1992) *(£5.00)*

The Probation Alternative - A Study Of The Impact of Four Enhanced Probation Schemes On Sentencing: Anne Creamer, Linda Hartley and Bryan Williams. (1992) *(£5.00)*

Evaluation of Compulsory Competitive Tendering for Local Authority Services : Richard Evans. (1992) *(£4.00)*

The Review of Residential Child Care in Scotland - The Three Supporting Research Studies : Andrew Kendrick, Sandy Fraser, Moira Borland and Juliet Harvey. (1992) *(£5.00)*

Education in and out of School - The Issues and the Practice in Inner Cities and Outer Estates : John MacBeath. (1992) *(£5.50)*

The Use of Judicial Separation : Alison Platts. (1992) *(£4.00)*

Policing in the City - Public, Police and Social Work : Richard Kinsey. (1993) *(£4.50)*

Counting Travellers in Scotland - The 1992 Picture : Hugh Gentleman. (1993) *(£4.50)*

Crime Prevention and Housebreaking in Scotland: David McAllister, Susan Leitch and Douglas Payne. (1993) *(£4.00)*

Supporting Victims of Serious Crime: Rebbecca Dobash, Pat McLauglin and Russell Dobash. (1993) *(£4.00)*

Prohibiting the Consumption of Alcohol in Designated Areas: Janet Ruiz. (1993) *(£4.50)*

Appeals in the Scottish Criminal Courts: Ann Millar. (1993) *(£4.50)*

The Attitudes of Young Women Drivers to Road Safety: Cragg, Ross & Dawson Ltd. (1993) *(£5.00)*

The Management of Child Abuse - A Longitudinal Study of Child Abuse in Glasgow: Ann Laybourn and Juliet Harvey. (1993) *(£5.00)*

Supporting Victims in the Criminal Justice System - A study of a Scottish sheriff Court: Rosemary I Wilson. (1993) *(£4.00)*

Consideration of the Mental State of Accused Persons at the Pre-Trial and Pre-Sentencing Stages: G. D.L. Cameron, J. J. McManus. (1993) *(£4.00)*

Process & Preference - Assessment of Older People for Institutional Care: Elaine Samuel, Sue Brace, Graham Buckley and Susan Hunter. (1993) *(£5.50)*

Untying the Knot: Characteristics of Divorce in Scotland: Sue Morris, Sheila Gibson and Alison Platts. (1993) *(£5.00)*

The Practice of Arbitration in Scotland 1986-1990: Dr Fraser P Davidson. (1993) *(£5.00)*

Police Specialist Units for the Investigation of Crimes of Violence Against Women and Children In Scotland: Ms M Burman and Ms S Lloyd. (1993) *(£5.00)*

Local Authority Housing Waiting Lists in Scotland: Sarah Dyer. (1993) *(£4.50)*

The Right to Buy in Scotland - An Assessment of the Impact of the First Decade of the Right to Buy: Karen MacNee. (1993) *(£4.00)*

A Better Start - Social Work Service Projects for Homeless Young People (1993): Anne Conner and Debbie Headrick.
Part 1: The Experience of The Scottish Office Rooflessness Report
Part 2: The Scottish Office Rooflessness Initiative - Background and Research Findings

The Effects of Privatisation of the Scottish Bus Group and Bus Deregulation: Consultant's Report by The Transport Operations Research Group, Newcastle University. (1993) *(£3.00)*

The Voluntary Sector and the Environment: Alistair McCulloch, Seaton Baxter and John Moxen. (1993) *(£3.00)*

Social Work Responses to the Misuse of Alcohol - A Literature Review: Murray Simpson, Bryan Williams and Andrew Kendrick. (1993) *(£4.50)*

Socio - legal Research in the Scottish Courts Vol 3 : (eds)Michael Adler, Ann Millar & Sue Morris (1993)*(£5.00)*

Review of Retailing Trends: John Dawson. (1994) *(£7.50)*

Empty Public Sector Dwellings in Scotland - A Study of Empty Public Sector Housing in Scotland in 1992: Alan Murie, Sally Wainwright and Keith Anderson, School of Planning and Housing, Edinburgh College of Art/ Heriot-Watt University. (1994) *(£5.50)*

An Evaluation of "Cars Kill" Television Commercial:
Research carried out on behalf of the Scottish Road Safety
Campaign by System Three Scotland. (1994) *(£5.00)*

**The Code of Guidance on Homelessness in Scotland -
Local Authority Policies and Practice:**Richard Evans,
Nicholas Smith, Caroline Bryson and Nicola Austin. (1994)
(£6.50)

**Operating Bail - Decision Making Under the Bail etc.
(Scotland) Act 1980:** Fiona Paterson and Claire Whittaker.
(1994) *(£15.95 from HMSO)*

Literature Review of Rural Issues: Karen MacNee.
(1994) *(£5.00)*

Review of Scottish Coastal Issues: Consultant's Report by
Peter R Burbridge and Veronica Burbridge. (1994) *(£5.00)*

**Detention and Voluntary Attendance of Suspects at
Police Stations:** The MVA Consultancy. (1994) *(£5.00)*

Police User Surveys in Scotland: Dr Nicholas R Fyfe.
(1994) *(£5.00)*

**Evaluation of The Scottish Road Safety Campaign's
Initiatives in Relation to the Year of the Eldery :**
Resarch carried out on behalf of the Scottish Road Safety
Campaign by the MVA Consultancy. (1994) *(£5.00)*

**Criminal Justice and Related Services for Young Adult
Offenders :** Stewart Asquith and Elaine Samuel. (1994)
(£11.95 from HMSO)

Neighbourhood Disputes in the Criminal Justice System:
R. E. MacKay and S.R. Moody with Fiona Walker.
(1994) *(£5.00)*

**Attitudes of Scottish Drivers Towards Speeding - 1994
Survey :** A Survey of Scottish Drivers conducted by Market
Research Scotland Ltd on behalf of the Scottish Office.
(1994) *(£5.00)*

A Review Of the Use Classes Order : Janet Brand
(Strathclyde University) in association with David Bryce
and Niall McClure (James Barr & Son, Chartered
Surveyors). (1994) *(£5.00)*

Review of Census Applications : Pauline Martin.
(1994) *(£5.00)*

Monetary Penalties in Scotland : Linda Nicholson. (1994)
(£13.95 from HMSO)

Multi-Party Actions In Scotland : Dr. Christine Barker,
Professor Ian D Willock and Dr. James J McManus.
(1994) *(£5.00)*

ISSN 0950 2254
ISBN 0 7480 1065 3
Price £4.00

HMSO 084053 10/94